in love with **life**

OSHO

Extemporaneous talks given by Osho in
OSHO International Meditation Resort, Pune, India

in love with **life**

Reflections on Friedrich Nietzsche's
Thus Spake Zarathustra

Originally published as *Zarathustra: A God That Can Dance* and *Zarathustra: The Laughing Prophet*

Ten selected talks by Osho, given to a live audience. All of Osho's talks have been published in full as books, and are also available as original audio recordings. Audio recordings and the complete text archive can be found via the online OSHO Library at www.osho.com/library

Osho comments on extracts from *Thus Spake Zarathustra: A Book for Everyone and No One* by Friedrich Nietzsche, translated by R. J. Hollingdale (Penguin Classics 1961, reprinted with a new Introduction 1969). Copyright © R. J. Hollingdale, 1961, 1969.

OSHO MEDIA INTERNATIONAL
New York • Zurich • Mumbai
an imprint of
OSHO INTERNATIONAL
www.osho.com/oshointernational

Distributed by Publishers Group Worldwide
www.pgw.com

Library of Congress Catalog-In-Publication Data is available

Printed in India by Manipal Technologies Limited, Karnataka

ISBN: 978-1-938755-96-5
This title is also available in eBook format ISBN: 978-0-88050-600-7

contents

preface

I t is the destiny of the genius to be misunderstood. If a genius is not misunderstood, he is not a genius at all. If the common masses can understand, that means the person is speaking at the same level where ordinary intelligence is.

Friedrich Nietzsche is misunderstood, and out of this misunderstanding there has been tremendous disaster. But perhaps it was unavoidable. To understand a man like Nietzsche you have to have at least the same standard of consciousness, if not higher.

Adolf Hitler is so retarded that it is impossible to think that he can understand the meaning of Nietzsche; but he became the prophet of Nietzsche's philosophy. And according to his retarded mind he interpreted – not only interpreted, but acted according to those interpretations – and the Second World War was the result. When Nietzsche is talking about "will to power," it has nothing to do with the will to dominate. But that is the meaning the Nazis gave to it.

"The will to power" is diametrically opposite to the will to dominate. The will to dominate comes out of an inferiority complex. One wants to dominate others, just to prove to himself that he is not inferior – he is superior. But he needs to prove it. Without any proof he knows he is inferior; he has to cover it up by many, many proofs.

The really superior man needs no proof, he simply is superior. Does a rose flower argue about its beauty? Does the full moon bother about proving its gloriousness? The superior man simply knows it, there is no need for any proof; hence he has no will to dominate. He certainly has a "will to power," but then you have to make a very fine distinction. His will to power means that he wants to grow to his fullest expression. It has nothing to do with anybody else, its whole concern is the individual himself. He wants to blossom, to bring all the flowers that are hidden in his potential, to rise as high as possible in the sky. It is not even comparative, it is not trying to rise higher than others – it is simply trying to rise to its fullest potential. "Will to power" is absolutely individual. It wants to dance to the highest in the sky, it wants to have a dialogue with the stars, but it is not concerned with proving anybody inferior. It is not competitive, it is not comparative.

Adolf Hitler and his followers, the Nazis, have done so much harm to the world because they prevented the world from understanding Friedrich Nietzsche and his true meaning. And it was not only one thing; about every other concept too, they have the same kind of misunderstanding.

It is such a sad fate, one which has never befallen any great mystic or any great poet before Nietzsche. The crucifixion of Jesus or poisoning of Socrates are not as bad a fate as that which has befallen Friedrich Nietzsche – to be misunderstood on such a grand scale that Adolf Hitler managed to kill more than eight million people in the name of Friedrich Nietzsche and his philosophy. It will take a little time.... When Adolf Hitler and the Nazis and the second world war are forgotten, Nietzsche will come back to his true light. He is coming back.

But Friedrich Nietzsche has to be interpreted again, so that all the nonsense that has been put, by the Nazis, over his beautiful philosophy can be thrown away.

People understand according to their own level of consciousness. It was just a coincidence that Nietzsche fell into the hands of the Nazis. They needed a philosophy for war, and Nietzsche appreciates the beauty of the warrior. They wanted some idea for which to fight, and Nietzsche gave them a good excuse – for the superman. Of course, they immediately got hold of the idea of superman. The Nordic German Aryans were going to be Nietzsche's new race of man, the superman. They wanted to dominate the world, and Nietzsche was very helpful, because he was saying that man's deepest longing is "will to power." They changed it into will to dominate.

Now they had the whole philosophy: the Nordic German Aryans are the superior race because they are going to give birth to the superman. They have the will to power and they will dominate the whole world. That is their destiny – to dominate the inferior human beings. Obviously, the arithmetic is simple: the superior should dominate the inferior.

These beautiful concepts…Nietzsche could not ever have imagined they would become so dangerous and such a nightmare to the whole of humanity. But you cannot avoid being misunderstood, you cannot do anything about it. Once you have said something, then it all depends on the other person, what he is going to make of it.

But Nietzsche is so immensely important that he has to be cleaned of all the garbage that the Nazis have put on his ideas.

**

Even if Nietzsche had not written anything else but *Thus Spake Zarathustra,* he would have served humanity immensely, profoundly – more cannot be expected from any man – because Zarathustra had been almost forgotten. It was Nietzsche who brought him back, who again gave him birth, a resurrection. *Thus Spake Zarathustra* is going to be the Bible of the future.

Osho
from *The Golden Future and Books I Have Loved*

CHAPTER 1

buddha and zorba can meet

Prologue Part 1

When Zarathustra was thirty years old, he left his home and the lake of his home and went into the mountains. Here he had the enjoyment of his spirit and his solitude and he did not weary of it for ten years. But at last his heart turned – and one morning he rose with the dawn, stepped before the sun and spoke to it thus: Great star! What would your happiness be, if you had not those for whom you shine!

You have come up here to my cave for ten years: you would have grown weary of your light and of this journey, without me, my eagle and my serpent.

But we waited for you every morning, took from you your superfluity and blessed you for it.

Behold! I am weary of my wisdom, like a bee that has gathered too much honey; I need hands outstretched to take it.

I should like to give it away and distribute it, until the wise among men have again become happy in their folly and the poor happy in their wealth.

To that end, I must descend into the depths: as you do at the evening, when you go behind the sea and bring light to the

underworld too, superabundant star!
Like you, I must go down – as men, to whom I want to descend,
call it.
So bless me then, tranquil eye, that can behold without envy even
an excessive happiness!
Bless the cup that wants to overflow, that the waters may flow
golden from him and bear the reflection of your joy over all the
world!
Behold! This cup wants to be empty again, and Zarathustra wants
to be man again.
Thus began Zarathustra's down-going.

Friedrich Nietzsche is perhaps the greatest philosopher the world has known. He is also great in another dimension which many philosophers are simply unaware of: he is a born mystic.

His philosophy is not only of the mind, but is rooted deep in the heart, and some roots reach even to his very being. The only thing unfortunate about him is that he was born in the West; hence, he could never come across any mystery school. He contemplated deeply, but he was absolutely unaware about meditation. His thoughts sometimes have the depth of a meditator, sometimes the flight of a Gautam Buddha; but these things seem to have happened spontaneously to him.

He knew nothing about the ways of enlightenment, about the path that reaches to one's own being. This created a tremendous turmoil in his being. His dreams go as high as the stars, but his life remained very ordinary. It does not have the aura that meditation creates. His thoughts are not his blood, his bones, his marrow. They are beautiful, immensely beautiful, but something is missing. What is missing is life itself. They are dead words, they don't breathe, there is no heartbeat.

But I have chosen to speak on him for a special reason: he is the only philosopher, from East or West, who has at least thought of the heights of human consciousness. He may not have experienced them; he certainly has not experienced them. He also thought of becoming a man again: that idea, of descending from your heights into the marketplace, descending from the stars to the earth, has never happened to anybody else.

He has something of Gautam Buddha, perhaps unconsciously

carried over from his past lives, and he has something of the Zorba; both are incomplete. But he is the only proof that Buddha and Zorba can meet; that those who have reached to the highest peaks need not remain there.

In fact, they should not remain there. They owe something to humanity; they owe something to the earth. They have been born amongst human beings, they have lived in the same darkness and in the same misery. And now that they have seen the light, it becomes obligatory that they should come back to wake up those who are fast asleep, to bring the good news – that darkness is not all, that unconsciousness is our choice.

If we choose to be conscious, all unconsciousness and all darkness can disappear. It is our choice that we are living in the dark valleys. If we decide to live on the sunlit peaks, nobody can prevent us because that is also our potential.

But the people who have reached to the sunlit peaks completely forget about the world they are coming from. Gautam Buddha never descended. Mahavira never descended. Even if they have made efforts for humanity to wake up, they have shouted from their sunlit peaks.

Man is so deaf, so blind that it is almost impossible for him to understand people who are talking from higher stages of consciousness. He hears the noise but it does not bring any meaning to him.

Nietzsche is unique in this sense. He could have remained an extraordinary, very superhuman philosopher, but he never forgets for a single moment the ordinary human being. It is his greatness. Although he has not touched the highest peaks and he has not known the greatest mysteries, whatsoever he has known, he is longing to share with his fellow human beings. His desire to share is tremendous.

I have chosen to speak on a few fragments that may be helpful to you for your spiritual growth. Nietzsche himself had chosen Zarathustra to be his spokesman. Something about Zarathustra has also to be understood. Amongst thousands of great mystics, philosophers, enlightened people, Nietzsche has chosen a very unknown person as his spokesman, almost forgotten to the world – Zarathustra.

The followers of Zarathustra are limited only to a small place – Mumbai. They had come to Mumbai from Iran when Mohammedans forced Persians either to be converted into Mohammedanism, or to be ready to be killed. Thousands were killed. Millions became

Mohammedans out of fear, but a few daring souls escaped from Iran
and landed in India.

They are the Parsis of Mumbai, perhaps the smallest religion
in the world. And it is amazing that Nietzsche was so interested in
Zarathustra that he wrote the book, *Thus Spake Zarathustra*. These
fragments are from that book.

He chose Zarathustra for the same reason that I chose him:
Zarathustra, amongst all the religious founders, is the only one who
is life affirmative; who is not against life, whose religion is a religion
of celebration, of gratefulness to existence. He is not against the
pleasures of life, and he is not in favor of renouncing the world. On
the contrary, he is in absolute support of rejoicing in the world
because except for this life and this world, all are hypothetical ideologies. God, heaven and hell, are all projections of the human
mind, not authentic experiences; they are not realities.

Zarathustra was born twenty five centuries ago, at a time when
all over the world there was a great renaissance. In India: Gautam
Buddha, Mahavira, Goshalak, Sanjay Vilethiputta, Ajit Keshkambal,
and others, had reached the same peak of awakening. In China:
Confucius, Mencius, Lao Tzu, Chuang Tzu, Lieh Tzu and many others.
In Greece: Socrates, Pythagoras, Heraclitus. And in Iran: Zarathustra.

It is a strange coincidence that suddenly, all over the world, there
came a flood of consciousness and many people became awakened. Perhaps enlightenment is also a chain reaction – when there
are enlightened people they provoke the same revolution in others.

It is everybody's potential. One just needs a provocation, a
challenge. When you see so many people reaching such beautiful
heights of grace you cannot remain where you are. Suddenly a great
urge arises in you: "Something has to be done. I am wasting my life
while others have reached the very destiny, have known all that
is worth knowing, have experienced the greatest blissfulness and
ecstasy. And what am I doing? – collecting seashells on the beach."

Out of all these people, Zarathustra is unique. He is the only one
who is not against life, who is for life; whose god is not somewhere
else, whose god is nothing but another name for life itself. And to
live totally, to live joyously and to live intensely, is all that religion is
based on.

I feel a deep empathy, affinity, with Zarathustra. But perhaps
because he was life affirmative and not life negative, he could not

gather many followers. It is one of the strange things about human beings: anything that is easy, they cannot accept as worthy of being the goal – the goal has to be very difficult and arduous.

Behind it is the psychology of the ego. The ego always wants something impossible because only with the impossible can it exist. You will never be able to fulfill desire, and the ego will go on pushing you toward more and more: more greed, more power, more money, more austerities, more spirituality, more discipline. Wherever you find *more*, remember, that is the language of the ego. And there is no way to satisfy the ego, it is always asking for more.

Zarathustra's whole approach is exactly the same as Chuang Tzu: "Easy is right. Right is easy." And when you are utterly relaxed, at ease, at home, so relaxed that you have even forgotten that you are at ease, that you have forgotten that you are right, you have become so utterly innocent like a child – you have arrived. But ego has no interest in this. This whole process is something like the suicide of the ego. Hence, religions which have been giving the ego difficult tasks, arduous paths, unnatural ideals, impossible goals, have attracted millions of people.

Zarathustra's followers can be counted on the fingers. Nobody has bothered about Zarathustra, until after almost twenty-four centuries, Nietzsche suddenly picked up on him. Nietzsche was against Jesus Christ and he was against Gautam Buddha, but he was for Zarathustra.

It is something very significant to understand. The man who was against Jesus Christ, against Gautam Buddha; why should he be for Zarathustra? – because Nietzsche also has the same attitude and approach toward life. He has seen all these religions, great religions, creating more and more guilt in humanity. Creating more and more misery, wars, burning people alive. Talking all kinds of nonsense for which no proof exists at all, for which they don't have any evidence at all. Keeping the whole of humanity in darkness, in blindness because their teachings are based on belief – and belief means blindness.

There is no belief which is not blind. A man with eyes does not believe in light, he knows it. There is no need to believe. Only the blind man believes in light because he does not know it. Belief exists in ignorance, and all the religions – with a few exceptions like Zarathustra and Chuang Tzu who have not been able to create great followings or great traditions – are all for belief. In other words, they are all for blindness.

Nietzsche was against them symbolically. As far as the East is concerned, he chose Gautam Buddha as the symbol and as far as the West is concerned, he chose Jesus Christ as the symbol. He was against these people for the simple reason that they were against life. They were against people enjoying the simple things: people living playfully, laughingly; people having a sense of humor, not seriousness. People loving songs and music, and people capable of dance and love.

Nietzsche was attracted to Zarathustra because he could see that this man alone, out of the whole past, was not against life; he was not against love, he was not against laughter.

In these fragments, you will see tremendously meaningful statements which can become the foundation of a life-affirmative religion. I am all for life. There is nothing for which life can be sacrificed. Everything can be sacrificed for life. Everything can be a means toward life, but life is an end unto itself.

Listen very carefully because Friedrich Nietzsche writes in a very condensed form. He is not a writer, he writes aphorisms. Anybody could have written a whole book but Nietzsche will write only one paragraph. His writing is so condensed that unless you are very alert in listening, you may miss. It is not to be read like a novel.

These are almost like the sutras of the Upanishad. Each single sutra, and each single maxim, contains so much, has so many implications. I would like to go into all the implications so that you do not misunderstand Nietzsche because he is one of the most misunderstood philosophers in the world. The reason for his being misunderstood is that he wrote in such a condensed form – he never explained, he never went into detailed explanations about all the possible implications.

He is a very symbolic man. The reason why he was so symbolic is that he was so full of new insights that there was not time enough to explain. He could not write treatises, and he had so much to share and to give, and life is so small.

Because his work was so condensed and crystallized, people in the first place did not understand him. In the second place, if they understood, they misunderstood. In the third place, they found him unreadable; they wanted everything to be explained. Nietzsche was not writing for children, he was writing for mature people. But maturity is so rare – the average mental age is not more than fourteen, and with this mental age Nietzsche is certainly going to be missed. He is missed by his opponents, and he is missed by his followers because both have the same mental age.

When Zarathustra was thirty years old, he left his home and the lake of his home and went into the mountains.

It has to be explained to you that Gautam Buddha left his palace when he was twenty-nine years old. Jesus started his teachings when he was thirty years old. Zarathustra went into the mountains when he was thirty years old. There is something significant about the age of thirty, or nearabout, just as at the age of fourteen one becomes sexually mature. If we take life as it has been taken traditionally, that it consists of seventy years, those who have watched life very deeply have found that every seven years, there is a change, a turning.

The first seven years are innocent. The second seven years, the child is very interested in inquiring, in questioning – curiosity. After the fourteenth up to the twenty-first year, he has the most powerful sexuality. The highest peak of sexuality, you will be surprised to know, is nearabout eighteen or nineteen years. And humanity has been trying to avoid that period by providing educational programs, colleges, universities – keeping boys and girls apart. That is the time when their sexuality and their sexual energy is at the highest point.

In those seven years, from fourteen to twenty-one, they could have experienced sexual orgasm very easily. Sexual orgasm is a glimpse, which can create in you the urge to find more blissful spaces. In sexual orgasm two things disappear: your ego disappears, your mind disappears – and time stops, just for a few seconds.

But these three are the important things. Two things disappear completely: you are no longer "I" – you are, but there is no sense of the ego. Your mind is there but there are no thoughts, just a deep stillness. Suddenly because the ego disappears and the mind stops, time stops too. To experience time, you need changing thoughts of the mind otherwise you cannot experience the movement of time.

Just think of two trains moving into empty space together at the same speed. Whenever you look out of the window at the other train – which has the same window and the same number of compartments

– you will not experience that you are moving. Neither will the passengers in the other train experience that they are moving.

You experience movement because when your train is moving, the trees are standing still, the houses are standing still; they are not moving. Stations come and platforms come and pass. It is because on both sides things are static that against them, in relativity, you can feel your train moving.

Sometimes you may have experienced a very bizarre thing: your train is standing on the platform, and another train is standing by the side. Your train starts moving. You are looking at the other train and it seems as if it has started moving, unless you look toward the platform, which is standing still. Movement is a relative experience.

When mind is not having any thoughts, you are in an empty sky. Time stops because you cannot judge time without movement – you are not there, mind is not there, time is not there…only a tremendous peace and a great relaxation.

My own understanding is that it was the sexual orgasm that gave the first idea to people about meditation. A few geniuses must have tried: "If we can stop thoughts, if we can drop the ego and if the mind is not there, time disappears. Then there is no need for any sexual orgasm." You can have the same orgasmic experience alone and it is no longer sexual – it becomes a spiritual experience.

Sexual orgasm must have given the first idea that the same experience is possible without sex. Otherwise, there is no way that man could have found meditation. Meditation is not a natural phenomenon. Sexual orgasm is a natural phenomenon, but all societies prevent their children from experiencing it. Nobody says anything about it. This is a strategy, a very dangerous strategy, a criminal act against the whole of humanity because the children who are deprived of having sexual orgasm will never be able to feel the urge for meditation; or their urge will be very weak, they will not risk anything for it.

So at the age twenty-one, sex reaches to its peak, if it is allowed as it was allowed in Gautam Buddha's life. All the beautiful girls of his kingdom were given to him; he was surrounded by them, he knew deep experiences of orgasm.

Then from twenty-one to twenty-eight, the other seven years, one searches because sexual orgasm is biological. Soon you will lose the energy and you will not be able to have an orgasm.

Secondly, it is dependent on somebody else, a woman, a man. It is destructive of your freedom; it is at a very high cost. So if a man grows very naturally – is allowed to grow naturally – from twenty-one to twenty-eight, he will search and seek ways and means to transcend physiology, biology, and yet remain capable of moving into deeper orgasmic experiences.

From twenty-eight to the age thirty-five, Gautam Buddha, Zarathustra, Lao Tzu, Chuang Tzu, Jesus, have all moved in higher planes of being. And just not to be bothered, not to be hindered by people, not to be distracted, they moved into the mountains – into aloneness. According to me, it was not against life – they were simply searching for a silent space where there were no distractions and they could find the greatest orgasmic experience. What William James has called "the oceanic orgasm," in which you completely disappear into the ocean of existence, just like a dewdrop slipping from a lotus leaf into the ocean.

So the age thirty is not just incidental. All great seekers have left in the search between twenty-eight and thirty-five. That is the period of seeking, searching – searching something that is not of the body, but of the spirit.

Here he had the enjoyment of his spirit and his solitude and he did not weary of it for ten years.

He remained in the mountains for ten years. His solitude, silence, peace, became deeper and deeper and he was full of bliss. Although he was alone, he was not weary of it.

But at last his heart turned – and one morning he rose with the dawn, stepped before the sun, and spoke to it thus...

This is where Zarathustra takes a new path. Mahavira remained in his solitude. Buddha remained in his aloneness, and the people who were watching, saw something had happened, something beyond their conceptions. These people were transformed. They had become luminous. They were radiating joy. They had a certain fragrance; they had known something. Their eyes had a depth that was not there before, and their faces had a grace that was a totally new phenomenon.

A very subtle misunderstanding happened. The people who were watching thought that because these people went into the mountains, they had renounced life. Hence, renouncing life became a fundamental thing in all the religions. But they had not renounced life.

I would like to rewrite history completely from scratch, particularly about these people because I know them from my own insight. I don't have to be bothered about facts; I know the truth. These people had not gone against life; they had gone simply for solitude, they had gone for being alone, they had just gone away from distractions.

But the difference between Gautam Buddha and Zarathustra is that Gautam Buddha – once he had found himself – never declared, "Now there is no need for me to be a recluse, to be a monk. I can come back and be an ordinary man in the world."

Perhaps it needs more courage than going out of the world; coming back to the world needs more courage. Going uphill is arduous, but very gratifying. You are going higher and higher and higher. And once you have reached to the highest peak, it needs tremendous courage to come back downward into the dark valleys which you had left, just to give the message to people: "You need not remain always in darkness. You need not remain always in suffering and in hell."

This downward journey may even be condemned by those people whom you are going to help. When you were going upward, you were a great saint, and when you are coming downward, people will think perhaps you have fallen, you have fallen from your greatness, from your height. It certainly needs the greatest courage in the world, after touching the heights of the ultimate, to be again ordinary.

Zarathustra shows that courage. He is not worried about what people will say, that he will be condemned, that they will think that he has fallen from heights, that he is no longer a saint. His concern is more to share his experience with those who may be ready, receptive, available – they may be few.

...and one morning he rose with the dawn, stepped before the sun, and spoke to it thus:
Great star! What would your happiness be, if you had not those for whom you shine!

The implication of this statement is great. Zarathustra is saying that the birds are happy because the sun has risen. The flowers are happy because the sun has risen. The whole planet seems to be happy, awake, full of energy, full of hope for the coming day – the sun has risen.

He is indicating in this statement that the sun also must be happy because so many flowers have blossomed, so many birds are singing. If there were no birds and no flowers, and there was nobody waiting for it, the sun would have been sad.

The implication is clear: we are all interconnected, the whole existence is interconnected. Even the smallest blade of grass is connected with the greatest star in the sky. Those connections are not visible.

It is known that if the sun does not rise one day, all life from the planet will disappear. Without the sun's heat and life-giving energy, nothing can remain alive here. But the mystics have always indicated about the other possibility too: if the whole of life disappears from the earth, the sun will not rise – for whom?

Zarathustra is saying, "I am full of joy, full of peace. Now I need somebody to receive it, I am overburdened. I have to share it, otherwise even blissfulness will become too heavy." Even blissfulness can become painful if unshared.

> Great star! What would your happiness be, if you had not those for whom you shine!
> You have come up here to my cave for ten years: you would have grown weary of your light and of this journey without me, my eagle and my serpent.

Zarathustra has two symbols: the eagle and the serpent. The serpent represents wisdom, and the eagle represents courage to fly into the unknown without any fear. He had with him the eagle and the serpent. One needs to be as conscious, as wise, as intelligent as possible. And one needs also the courage to go on entering into the unknown and finally into the unknowable. The jump into the unknowable is the jump into the godliness of existence.

> But we waited for you every morning, took from you your superfluity and blessed you for it.

Whatever you have given to us was superfluous to you, you had too much of it, you were burdened with it. You wanted somebody to share it and we have taken from your superfluous abundant energy, overflowing energy, and we have blessed you for it.

Behold! I am weary of my wisdom...

In the same way as you are weary of your light and you want somebody to share it, I am weary of my wisdom – it is too much. I cannot contain it anymore, I have to find someone to share. I have to unburden myself.

This is such a great insight – that even wisdom can become a burden. Zarathustra is absolutely right.

...like a bee that has gathered too much honey; I need hands outstretched to take it.
I should like to give it away and distribute it, until the wise among men have again become happy in their folly...

This can be said only by someone who has known. An ordinary person who is simply learned, who has borrowed knowledge, cannot even conceive the idea.

Nietzsche is saying through Zarathustra: "I am going amongst men to share, to distribute and to unburden myself of my wisdom until the wise among men have again become happy in their folly."

The truly wise man is not serious, he is playful because he understands that the whole of existence is playful. The truly wise man may appear to people somewhat crazy, foolish because ordinary humanity has a fixed idea of the wise man: that he is serious, that he cannot be playful, that he cannot laugh, that he cannot dance.

These things are for foolish people. Zarathustra is saying, "I will go on sharing my wisdom until the wise amongst men have become so wise that they can accept even things which look foolish to the ordinary man."

...and the poor happy in their wealth.

As far as the inner wealth is concerned, the poor man is as endowed by nature as any rich man. The rich man is too engaged with the outside world and perhaps may not find the way or the time to enter inward. But the poor man is in a fortunate condition, he has nothing to be engaged with on the outside, he can close his eyes and go in. Zarathustra is saying that unless the wise are so wise that even foolishness becomes just playfulness, and the poor are so happy as if they have found the greatest treasure...

> *To that end, I must descend into the depths: as you do at the evening, when you go behind the sea and bring light to the underworld too, superabundant star!*
> *Like you, I must go down – as men, to whom I want to descend, call it.*
> *So bless me then, tranquil eye, that can behold without envy, even an excessive happiness!*
> *Bless the cup that wants to overflow, that the waters may flow golden from him and bear the reflection of your joy over all the world!*
> *Behold! This cup wants to be empty again, and Zarathustra wants to be man again.*

This is the rare quality of Zarathustra. There have been thousands of men who wanted to be supermen – who wanted to be Buddhas, Jainas, Christs, avatars – but Zarathustra, alone in the whole of history, wants to be a man again. Seeing the heights, seeing the depths, knowing the ultimate solitude, being full of wisdom, he wants to go down and be just a man amongst men – not anybody superior.

Thus began Zarathustra's down-going.

This *down-going* of Zarathustra is so unique and so significant that unless every wise man has the same courage, humanity's destiny cannot be changed.

If all the Gautam Buddhas and all the Jesus Christs, all the Moseses and all the Mohammeds, had come back to humanity just as men; they would have given dignity to humanity, they would have given great courage to humanity, they would have become sources of great inspiration. But they are far above; the distance is so great that it creates discouragement. Not only they, but their disciples have been trying in every possible way to create more and more distance.

For example, Jesus was born of a virgin girl: it is a discouragement to the whole of humanity because you are born out of sin, and
only Jesus is not born out of sin. If he is the only begotten son of
God, then who are you? You are not even cousins!

Why is God so miserly that he should have only one son? Did he
believe in birth control? The Christians are against it. At least one
daughter was a must! But to dishonor womankind, God cannot have
a daughter, nor has he a wife; but he has a son. His son walks on
water; you cannot do it. He brings dead people back to life; you
cannot do that. He is crucified but he comes back again – resurrection; you cannot manage that.

Naturally, the distance is too great. You are a mere human
being; he is a god. At the most, you can worship him. He is a humil-
iation to you. He is a great insult to the whole of humanity. And all
these miracles are fictitious. Nobody has ever done those miracles,
but just to create the distance between you and Jesus, their followers have gone to extreme lengths.

Mohammed dies, but not like an ordinary man. In fact, he does
not die in the way people die – he simply goes directly to heaven,
alive. And not only he alone, he is riding on his horse, so the horse
also goes directly into paradise. It is no ordinary horse – it is Hazrat
Mohammed's horse. You cannot think of yourself belonging to the
same category.

Mahavira never perspired. In the hot summers of India – and
particularly in Bihar, on dusty roads – he was moving naked for
forty-two years, and he did not perspire! It is possible only if his
body was not covered with skin but with plastic – because the body
is covered with skin and the skin breathes and perspiration is a very
necessary process for your survival; otherwise you will die.

Perspiration is a protection. When it is too hot, your pores start
bringing water out of the body so that the heat is engaged in evapo-
rating your perspiration and does not increase your temperature; your
temperature remains the same. If the body does not perspire, your temperature will go on rising higher and higher. And you don't have much
of a range – between ninety-eight degrees and one hundred and ten.
Just twelve degrees more and Mahavira would have popped out; he
could not have stayed alive. But just to make a difference, he did not
take a bath; there was no need. When he did not perspire, there was
no need for taking a shower.

A snake bites him and instead of blood, milk comes out. I was speaking at a Jaina conference and just before me, a Jaina monk had spoken. He had praised all these miracles of Mahavira and when I spoke, I said, "These were not miracles. Just a little thinking will make it clear that milk can come out from the feet only if, instead of blood, milk is circulating in Mahavira's body. But for forty-two years, milk circulating would have become curd, would have become butter, would have even become ghee. It remained milk! Fresh milk came out!

"The other possibility is that just as milk comes from a woman's breast – but the breast has a subtle mechanism to transform blood into milk. This was also possible, if you insist that all over his body Mahavira had milk-creating systems."

But this is nonsense. And yet everybody... Gautam Buddha is born while his mother is standing up, and it can be tolerated because it is not much of a problem. Perhaps the mother was a little crazy or something; otherwise, when the child is being born, the mother must be lying on the bed – not standing. But one can accept that maybe the woman was crazy. But Gautam Buddha is himself born standing; he falls on the ground – standing. That too some-times happens. Ordinarily, the head comes first but once in a while a child is born with feet first. If the story stops there it is feasible, but it will not make a great impression on you.

But Buddha walked seven feet! A newly born child, in fact, cannot stand, but he walked seven feet. And not only walked, after seven feet he looked at the sky and declared, "I am the greatest buddha, the greatest enlightened man, past, present, future."

Now these are great discouragements: you cannot manage these things. In the first place, you are already born. You can try next time, but this life is gone. In this life you cannot become an awakened person, so just practice for the second life. Remember, exactly what has to be done.

But all these things, these fictions have a particular purpose. The purpose is to make these people so far away from human beings that you can at the most worship them, but you cannot even dream that the same experience can happen to you.

What Zarathustra did should be done by every enlightened person. Every enlightened person should come back to the world. He owes it to the world. He is indebted to humanity. He is born a human child and he cannot be forgiven for creating myths around himself, or letting other people create myths around him so that he becomes something impossible.

Zarathustra is more human, more lovable and one can see his point in coming back to humanity. He has gathered so much wisdom, so much honey, he wants to share it – to distribute it. He wants himself to be empty again because now he knows that the more he gives, the more existence will go on pouring into him. He can go on emptying himself and still he will have an abundance to share.

A man who is in authentic love with humanity, a man who affirms life, is not condemnatory, is not negative; he does not make anybody feel guilty. On the contrary, he helps everybody: "Whatever I have is hidden within you too." His coming down is nothing but to encourage those who are ready, those who are in need of some guidance, those who want to know the path, those who want to experience their innermost treasure.

Zarathustra should be more and more understood for the benefit of the coming humanity. He is more of a blessing than anybody else.

...Thus spake Zarathustra.

CHAPTER 2

wisdom brings authentic freedom

Prologue Part 2

Zarathustra went down the mountain alone, and no one met him. But when he entered the forest, an old man, who had left his holy hut to look for roots in the forest, suddenly stood before him. And the old man spoke thus to Zarathustra:

"This wanderer is no stranger to me: he passed by here many years ago. He was called Zarathustra; but he has changed.

"Then you carried your ashes to the mountains: will you today carry your fire into the valleys? Do you not fear an incendiary's punishment?

"Yes, I recognize Zarathustra. His eyes are clear, and no disgust lurks about his mouth. Does he not go along like a dancer?

"How changed Zarathustra is! Zarathustra has become – a child, an awakened-one: what do you want now with the sleepers?

"You lived in solitude as in the sea, and the sea bore you. Alas, do you want to go ashore? Alas, do you want again to drag your body yourself?"

Zarathustra answered: "I love mankind."

"Why," said the saint, "did I go into the forest and the desert? Was it not because I loved mankind all too much?

"Now I love God: mankind I do not love. Man is too imperfect a thing for me. Love of mankind would destroy me."
Zarathustra answered, "What did I say of love? I am bringing mankind a gift."
"Give them nothing," said the saint. "Rather take something off them and bear it with them – that will please them best; if only it be pleasing to you!
"And if you want to give to them, give no more than an alms, and let them beg for that!"
"No," answered Zarathustra, "I give no alms. I am not poor enough for that."
The saint laughed at Zarathustra and spoke thus:
"See to it that they accept your treasures! They are mistrustful of hermits, and do not believe that we come to give.
"Our steps ring too lonely through their streets. And when at night they hear in their beds a man going by long before the sun has risen, they probably ask themselves: where is that thief going?
"Do not go to men, but stay in the forest! Go rather to the animals! Why will you not be as I am – a bear among bears, a bird among birds?"
"And what does the saint do in the forest?' asked Zarathustra.
The saint answered: "I make songs and sing them, and when I make songs, I laugh, weep, and mutter: thus I praise God.
"With singing, weeping, laughing, and muttering I praise the God who is my God. But what do you bring us as a gift?"
When Zarathustra heard these words, he saluted the saint and said: "What should I have to give you!"
"But let me go quickly, that I may take nothing from you!" And thus they parted from one another, the old man and Zarathustra, laughing as two boys laugh.
But when Zarathustra was alone, he spoke thus to his heart:
"Could it be possible! This old saint has not yet heard in his forest that God is dead!"

Zarathustra had gone to the mountains in search of aloneness. In the crowd you can find yourself lonely, but never alone. Loneliness is a kind of hunger for the other. You are missing the other. You are not enough unto yourself – you are empty. Hence everybody wants to be in the crowd, and weaves around himself many kinds of relationships just to deceive himself, to forget that he is lonely. But that loneliness erupts again and again. No relationship can hide it. All relationships are so thin and so fragile. Deep inside you know perfectly well that even though you are in the crowd, you are amongst strangers. You are a stranger to yourself too.

Zarathustra and all the mystics have gone to the mountains in search of aloneness. Aloneness is a positive feeling, the feeling of your own being and the feeling that you are enough unto yourself, that you don't need anyone. Loneliness is a sickness of the heart. Aloneness is a healing.

Those who know aloneness have gone beyond loneliness forever. Whether they are alone or with people, they are centered within themselves. In the mountains they are alone, in the crowd they are alone because this is their realization: that aloneness is our nature. We have come into the world alone and we will be leaving the world again alone.

Between these two alonenesses, between birth and death, you are still alone. But you have not understood the beauty of aloneness, and hence you have fallen into a kind of fallacy – the fallacy of loneliness.

To discover one's aloneness one has to go out of the crowd. Slowly, slowly as he forgets the world, all his awareness becomes concentrated on himself, and there is an explosion of light. For the first time he comes to know the beauty and the blessing of being alone, the tremendous freedom and the wisdom of being alone.

Zarathustra used to carry a serpent and an eagle while he was living in the mountains. In the East, the serpent has always represented wisdom. The greatest wisdom is to go on slipping out of the past, without clinging to it, just like a serpent slips out of his old skin and never looks back. His movement is always from the old to the new.

Wisdom is not the collection of the past; wisdom is the experience of the constantly renewing life. Wisdom does not gather the dust of memories; it remains like a clean mirror, reflecting that which is – always fresh, always new, always in the present.

The eagle is a symbol of freedom. Alone, it goes across the sun, far away in the boundless sky, with no fear. Wisdom and freedom are two aspects of the same coin.

Living in the mountains for ten years, Zarathustra attained the ecstasy of being alone, the purity of being alone, the independence of being alone. This is where he is unique amongst other awakened people; when they discovered, they remained in their heights. Zarathustra starts *down-going*, going back to the crowd. He has to deliver the message to humanity: "You are suffering unnecessarily, you are being dependent unnecessarily, you are creating all kinds of imprisonments for yourself – just to feel safe and secure. But the only security and the only safety is in knowing yourself because then even death is impotent. It cannot destroy you."

Zarathustra is going downward from the mountains to tell the people that wisdom is not synonymous with knowledge. In fact, knowledge is just the opposite of wisdom. Wisdom is basically innocence, knowledge is ego, and wisdom is the disappearance of the ego. Knowledge makes you full of information. Wisdom makes you absolutely empty, but that emptiness is a new kind of fullness. It is a spaciousness.

He is going to the people to tell them that wisdom brings freedom. There is no other freedom: political, economical, social freedoms are all fake. The only authentic freedom is of the soul, which can become an eagle and go into the unknown and the unknowable without any fear.

Because he has attained this state of ultimate consciousness, he wants to share it. The uniqueness about him is that he still loves mankind. There is no condemnation about the sleeping people, the blind people. There is tremendous compassion for them. He is going downward because he loves life. He is not against life.

This small dialogue with an old saint who lives in the forest is very significant. It contains much which may not be apparent, but we will try to discover it as deeply as possible.

Zarathustra went down the mountain alone, and no one met him. But when he entered the forest, an old man, who had left his holy hut to look for roots in the forest, suddenly stood before him. And the old man spoke thus to Zarathustra:
"This wanderer is no stranger to me. He passed by here many years ago. He was called Zarathustra; but he has changed."

The old saint could see the change. Although it is the same man, it is not the same energy. It is the same man, but it is a totally different individual. He has gone into the mountains as ignorant, and he is coming out of the mountains as the wisest man possible. He has gone there asleep; he is coming back awakened. He has gone through a transformation.

When he went to the mountains he was just a mortal, and when he comes out of the mountains he has attained immortality. Now he is full of joy, full of peace, showering blessings all around him. He is overflowing with love, with compassion.

"Then you carried your ashes to the mountains..."

You were nothing but a corpse. And you had carried your ashes to the mountains.

"...will you today carry your fire into the valleys?"

The transformation has been so radical – instead of being ashes, he is now fire. He has gone as darkness, now he is aflame.

"Do you not fear an incendiary's punishment?"

This is significant to note. The old saint is saying, "Are you not afraid going back to the blind people, with eyes? Going to the dead, full of life? Going to the asleep, awakened?"

When you had come from them, you were one of them. Now you are totally different. Don't you think you are taking a risk? They will punish you. They will not forgive you. Your blissfulness is too much; they will not be able to tolerate it.

It is a strange fact: we can tolerate people's misery, however deep it is. We have a certain enjoyment when others are miserable because when they are miserable, you are higher than them. You can show sympathy and you can rejoice in the fact that you are not so miserable. Hence, no miserable person has ever been crucified, ever poisoned, ever stoned to death.

But to be blissful amongst miserable people is dangerous because you are a height, and they feel offended. You can see and they cannot. It is unbearable. They are dead and you are alive. You have to be punished. You have gone astray from the crowd. Are you not afraid of the punishment?

"Yes, I recognize Zarathustra. His eyes are clear, and no disgust lurks in his mouth. Does he not go along like a dancer?"

The eyes are very symbolic. They are part of your body, but they are also windows of your soul. As your soul becomes silent, peaceful, joyous, your eyes attain a depth, a clarity, a purity, an innocence. They become so transparent that you can see into the very soul of the man.

"His eyes are clear, and no disgust lurks in his mouth." If you look at people, they are disgusted with the whole of life and you cannot blame them. What have they got? Their whole life is nothing but a long-drawn-out tragedy. It is sickness unto death. They go on breathing, they go on living, they go on hoping. But those hopes always remain hopes. Their dreams are never fulfilled.

As they grow older, they see their hopes shattering more and more. It is natural that they will be full of disgust with this whole business of life. They had never asked to be born, they have never asked that they should be given a heart which feels, which needs warmth, which needs love.

They have never asked that they should be given a soul that longs for the ultimate heights of joy and ecstasy. They suddenly find themselves, and all that has been given to them by existence remains unfulfilled. They are truly angry.

One of the most significant novelists, Fyodor Dostoyevsky, in his great novel *Brothers Karamazov*, has one character who says, "I have only one relationship with God, and that is of disgust. I am angry, and if I can meet him, the only thing I am going to do is to give him the ticket back and ask him to find the way out of life. It is a cruel joke. He gives us so many desires, so many longings, and there is no opportunity to fulfill them. There is not even any hope in the future." Everybody is born with great enthusiasm, and everybody dies just frustrated.

The old saint says, "Now I don't see any disgust, any agony; instead I see ecstasy. He goes along like a dancer." You had come to the mountains dragging yourself somehow, carrying your own corpse on your shoulders, and now: *"Does he not go along like a dancer?"*

The transformation has happened. The man has realized himself. The man has drunk from the sources of the divine.

"How changed Zarathustra is! Zarathustra has become – a child..."

That is the greatest change in life – to be a child again.

"...an awakened-one: what do you want now with the sleepers?"

The question of the saint is the question of all the saints of the world, all the buddhas, all the mystics, all the awakened ones. You have become a child, you are awakened: *"...what do you want now with the sleepers?"* You are an absolute stranger to them. They will punish you, they may kill you. Your very presence will become a danger to their sleep, a danger to their misery, a danger to their blindness.

"You lived in solitude as in the sea, and the sea bore you. Alas, do you want to go ashore? Alas, do you want again to drag your body yourself?"

Have you forgotten the day you had come to the mountains? Do you want to be the same old self again? Why are you going down-ward, leaving your sunlit peaks? You know in the valleys there is darkness alone. What is the purpose of your going?

Zarathustra answered: "I love mankind."

In those three words is contained Zarathustra's whole philos-ophy: "I love mankind. I love life. I had not renounced the world. I had not come to the mountains as an antilife escapist. I had come to the mountains to find myself, my aloneness, my freedom, my wisdom. I have found it.

"Now there is no need for me to remain on the heights. On the contrary, I am so full that I need people to share with. I want to share my love, I want to share my wisdom, I want to share my freedom. I am too overloaded – I am overflowing."

"Why," said the saint, "did I go into the forest and the desert? Was it not because I loved mankind all too much?"

The saint says, "I have also gone into the mountains, into the forest because I loved mankind all too much. It has become a slavery, and it has become a dependence. It was bringing me only misery and nothing else."

But there is a difference. He loved mankind *...all too much...* when he was ignorant, when he himself was asleep. Zarathustra loves mankind when he is fully awake, when he is enlightened. The love of the unawakened is nothing but lust. Only the awakened knows the beauty and the spirituality, and the divinity of love. It is no longer a bondage.

The love of the awakened gives you freedom.

The love of the unawakened is that of a beggar's love: he wants you to love him, he wants to give more and more love. The love of the awakened is just the reverse. It is the love of an emperor. He wants to give to you – he has so much, such an abundance. It is giving, it is sharing without any desire to be rewarded and without any desire to get anything in return.

The saint said:

"Now I love God: mankind I do not love."

In this statement is contained the whole attitude of all the so-called religions. They have been creating a division that if you love mankind you cannot love God. The Old Testament God says, "I am very jealous. If you love me, you cannot love anyone else."

That is the attitude of almost all religions. Either you can love this world, then you have renounced the other world; if you love man, you have forgotten God. You can choose. If you love God, you will have to withdraw your love from mankind. In fact, you will have to hate mankind, you will have to hate life, you will have to hate all the pleasures of life. This idea of religions is very monopolistic. God wants the love in your heart in its totality. He cannot tolerate any competitor.

"Now I love God: mankind I do not love. Man is too imperfect a thing for me. Love of mankind would destroy me."

Through the old saint, the whole religious attitude of antilife, anti-joy, anti-pleasure is condensed. Why can you not love mankind? – because mankind is too imperfect a thing. God is perfect. *"Love of mankind would destroy me."*

The reality is that love in its purity, in its spiritual flowering, does not make any distinction. It loves, not because you are worthy; it loves, not because you are perfect; it loves, not because you are God – true love loves for love's sake. The object of love is irrelevant. You are so full of love that you go on sharing with those who are imperfect. And, in fact, they need more. Those who are unworthy, in fact, need more. Those who are undeserving, in fact, need more.

The perfect God has no need of your love – the perfect God is only a hypothesis, it is only in your mind. You have never come across him; otherwise, a man who goes on looking for imperfections will find imperfections in God, too.

Have you ever thought about it? If God suddenly appears in front of you, will you not be able to find imperfections in him? – you will find imperfections in him too. Perhaps he is not as beautiful as you had imagined. Perhaps he looks Chinese, or perhaps he is a Negro, or perhaps he is a Negro woman! Perhaps he is too old, too ancient – there is no freshness around him, but only a stinking oldness, he has been there for centuries.

There are so many hypothetical conceptions of God. Some believe he has four hands. Do you think four hands will look right? And some think he has one thousand hands. A man with one thousand hands will be perfectly useful to be kept in a museum, but to love him... And if he gives you a hug – with one thousand hands! Once you can get out of his hug, you will never think of God again.

There are conceptions of God with three faces. It will be curious to see him, but a man with three faces will not look beautiful. And who knows what kind of faces those are?

The perfection of God is in your mind because God is only a mind projection. And you can love God very easily because there is no God, so there is no problem.

To love a woman or to love a man... There are problems. Your likings differ; your preferences differ. You want to go to a movie, and your wife insists on not going to the movie; she has a headache.

Once it was asked of Henry Ford: "How did you go on becoming richer and richer and richer; what was the motivation?" He said, "To tell you the truth, I wanted to see whether I can earn more than my wife can spend, and I have to accept that I am a failure."

With the other person there are problems. You want to sleep and your husband snores. What can you do with this husband who is just sleeping by your side, snoring? And he is helpless also. Thousands of methods have been tried to prevent snoring. The latest is an electrically engineered bag hanging over the husband's mouth. The moment he snores, the bag immediately falls on his face, and then he wakes up – would you let him sleep the whole night or not? – whenever he snores, the bag comes immediately over his nose and mouth, and closes them.

You have a wife whose body smell you cannot tolerate...

With God everything is beautiful because neither you have to sleep with him – let him snore – nor do you have to live with him. If his body stinks, let it stink. It is a pure hypothesis in your mind.

But to be in contact with real human beings is a totally different experience. It is a fire test for your love. It is very easy to love God; it is very difficult to love man. It costs nothing to love God; it needs tremendous understanding to love a man.

So those who have escaped into the forest and the mountains, and are projecting an idea of God, and love that God, have chosen a very easy kind of life. Their love is not going to grow because it has no challenges.

The old saint is speaking, almost in essence, of the whole approach of all religions: "Love of mankind will destroy me. Man is too imperfect a thing for me." This is egoistic. He thinks himself to be perfect and mankind is too imperfect a thing. Of course a perfect man can only love a perfect God – and God is just your hallucination. If you persist, you may see the God of your conception: it is nothing but a dream seen with open eyes – it is hallucinatory. There is nobody in front of you, but your own idea has hypnotized you.

That's why a Christian will see Jesus and a Buddhist will see Buddha and a Hindu will see Krishna. Even by mistake a Christian never sees Buddha or Krishna. Even by mistake Krishna never comes to a Christian, Christ never comes to a Hindu – because these people don't exist. They are part of your mind; you create them. The Bible says God created man in his own image. I say unto you: man creates God in his own image.

Zarathustra answered, "What did I say of love? I am bringing mankind a gift."

Love is always a gift; otherwise it is abstract poetry. *"What did I say of love? I am bringing mankind a gift."* The old saint is saying very significant things: "Give them nothing because they never forgive those people who give them anything."

Socrates gave people an immensely valuable method to find truth: the Socratic dialogue. But what did mankind do to him? – poisoned him.

The old saint has some truth when he is saying:

"Give them nothing... Rather take something off them and bear it with them – that will please them best; if only it be pleasing to you!"

It is part of human psychology that you want to be a giver; you don't want to be a receiver. But there are things which you have to receive. There is no way for you to give them because you don't have them.

What can you give to Gautam Buddha or to Jesus Christ or to Zarathustra? You are a beggar, but still the psychology is that you have to give them something, and that will make you happy. They may give you tremendous treasures, but you will never forgive them because they are the givers and you are the receivers. You are a beggar. How can you forgive someone who has made you a beggar?

I have a friend who was born poor, but was adopted by one of the richest families in India. He is a very generous man – he has made all his relatives rich, comfortable. He goes on giving to friends, to relatives, even to strangers. But he confessed to me once while traveling with me in the train: "I have always wanted to ask you something, but I could not gather courage to expose myself. I have given to all my relatives who were poor, and now they are rich people. I have given to my friends. I have even given to strangers who have asked. I have never said no to anybody – I have so much that I can go on giving. But they are all angry at me; they talk against me."

I said, "It is very simple: have you ever allowed them to give something to you?"

He said, "I don't need anything."

I said, "That explains everything. But small things... For example, you can phone a friend to whom you have given money, a factory, and made a man rich, and say: 'Just passing by your house I saw

beautiful roses in your garden. Will you bring me a few roses?' And
the friend's attitude toward you will change.

"If you are sick, you can phone somebody and say: 'I am lying in
bed with a bad headache and fever, and a great desire has arisen
in me for you, that you should be close to me. Just come here, hold
my hand and sit by my side.' That will be enough.

"You have many cars, but you could have told any of your relatives: 'I need your car for one day.' You don't have to use it. Just keep
it in the garage and by the evening return it. But your relative or your
friend will think he can also give something to you. He is also needed."

He said, "I will try, although I am very reluctant. I have made
them whatsoever they are. Why should I ask anything? I have roses
in my garden. I have my own cars, and their cars I have given to
them; their houses I have given to them."

I said, "It is up to you. It is your ego that is hurting them all – that
you are the giver, and they are always the receiver. If you want to
change their attitude toward you, you have to become in some way
a receiver. Let them enjoy for some moments the ego of giving."

He tried, and next time he met me, he said, "It works, it works
miracles! I had never seen! Those people are so happy with me.
They are talking about my generosity. Now that I am taking things
from them, I have become generous. Otherwise, they were always
saying, 'He is just an egoist; he has given to us not because we
needed anything, he has given just to humiliate us!'"

The old saint is right:

*"Give them nothing... Rather take something off them and bear it
with them – that will please them best; if only it be pleasing to you!
"And if you want to give to them, give no more than an alms, and
let them beg for that!"*

His advice is very significant and based on deep psychological
truths. Just give them alms. Don't give them too much. Give them
enough so that they start wanting more. Then they will always be
wagging their tail around you. Give them only when they beg, and
they will be happy with you because you have not reduced them
to beggars. They themselves have begged; it is not your fault, they
cannot be angry with you.

But a man like Zarathustra cannot do that.

*"No," answered Zarathustra, "I give no alms. I am not poor
enough for that!"*

A great statement: *"I am not poor enough for that!"* To reduce
somebody to begging, and to give in such little amounts that it creates the desire for more in them, shows my poverty. *I am not poor
enough for that!*

I have abundance: abundance of love, abundance of peace,
abundance of truth, abundance of wisdom, abundance of freedom;
and these things cannot be given in parts. They can be given only as
a whole. You cannot cut truth into pieces. You cannot cut love into
fragments. Either you give or you don't give. But if you give, you
have to give it wholeheartedly, with totality. It does not matter even if
they crucify you; it does not matter if they become irritated and
annoyed with you.

*The saint laughed at Zarathustra and spoke thus:
"See to it that they accept your treasures!"*

Because they have always been rejecting them. Deep down
they want the treasures, but when somebody comes to give them, they
reject them. There is a joy in rejecting: why have you rejected Buddha
or Mahavira or Jesus? By rejecting, you have shown them: "You may
have the treasure, but we are not so poor to accept it. You may be rich
in having it. We are rich, more rich than you, in rejecting it."

The old man's advice is based on great wisdom.

*"See to it that they accept your treasures! They are mistrustful of
hermits, and do not believe that we come to give.
"Our steps ring too lonely through the streets. And when at night
they hear in their beds a man going by long before the sun has
risen, they probably ask themselves: where is that thief going?
"Do not go to men, but stay in the forest! Go rather to the animals!"*

I have loved this advice of the old saint because animals are
innocent: they will not reject you, and they will not be annoyed with
you, and they will not crucify you.

I would just like to add to it: go to the animals, go to the trees – they are more sensitive. Man has become almost insensitive, and the higher the value, the more insensitive he is. He understands only the language of money, power, prestige. He has forgotten the language of love, the language of joy, the language of dance.

> *"Why will you not be as I am – a bear among bears, a bird among birds?"*
> *"And what does the saint do in the forest?" asks Zarathustra.*
> *The saint answered: "I make songs and sing them, and when I make songs, I laugh, weep, and mutter: thus I praise God.*
> *"With singing, weeping, laughing, and muttering I praise the God who is my God. But what do you bring us as a gift?"*
> *When Zarathustra heard these words, he saluted the saint and said: "What should I have to give you!*
> *"But let me go quickly, that I may take nothing from you!" And thus they parted from one another, the old man and Zarathustra, laughing as two boys laugh."*

Zarathustra said, *"What should I have to give to you!"* You sing, you create songs, you are joyous. In your aloneness you are absolutely happy. What can I give to you? Let me go, I am afraid I may take something from you, and I am already too burdened with songs, with blissfulness. We both are burdened. You have chosen to live with the bears as a bear, to live with the birds as a bird, to live with the trees as a tree. I have chosen to go back to man, and to live as a man. I have nothing to give to you. You have got it. They understood each other, and the old man and Zarathustra, laughing as two boys, parted from one another.

> *But when Zarathustra was alone, he spoke thus to his heart: "Could it be possible! This old saint has not yet heard in his forest that God is dead!"*

This is something to be understood by anybody who is in search of truth, in search of religiousness, in search of spiritual growth: that God is only a hypothesis. Saying that God is dead is only a way of saying that God has never been alive. It is just to satisfy man's curiosity that the cunning minds have invented the idea of God. It is not a revelation, it is just imagination, and forced by conditioning for centuries.

But in his heart he said: "Could it be possible that such a beautiful old man who makes songs and sings, who lives with birds and trees and animals, has not yet heard in his forest that God is dead? That he is still talking of loving God?"

With Zarathustra and with Friedrich Nietzsche I agree totally. Just my expression is different. I want to say that God has never been alive; there has never been any God. God is an invention out of fear, or out of greed, or out of frustrations in life. God is the invention of those who were not able to learn the art of life.

And because they could not dance, they started condemning dance. In fact they themselves were crippled because they could not live. Life needs alertness, intelligence, patience, tolerance. Because they could not create these qualities in themselves, they created the idea that life is something wrong: it has to be renounced. But you cannot renounce anything unless there is something bigger to gain by your renunciation. So God is the greatest projection of greed: renounce the world and you can get God. Renounce the world and you can get paradise.

These are the inventions of the escapists, of the crippled, of the retarded; of those who have not been able to learn the art of love, the art of living, who don't know how to sing, who don't know how to dance. Naturally, one who does not know how to dance will condemn dance. One who does not know how to sing will condemn singing. That is a defensive measure to hide one's retardation, to hide one's ignorance.

God is the creation of the unwise, not of the wise. It is the creation of the slaves, not of those who love freedom.

Zarathustra is immensely in love with life and all that life provides. He is the only mystic with immense affirmation of life. There is no place for renouncing anything – life is a gift of existence. Learn to enjoy it! Relish in it. Dance with the trees, and dance with the stars. Love without jealousy. Live without competition. Accept everybody without judgment. And then there is no need for any God. And there is no need for any paradise. We can transform this very earth into a divine existence. Our very life can become the expression of godliness.

I am all for godliness because godliness is a quality you can learn, you can grow. God is just a dead idea. The sooner it is dropped, the better because it unnecessarily wastes your time.

Millions of people are praying around the earth, not knowing that there is nobody to hear their prayers. Millions are worshipping stone statues. If they cannot love living human beings, how is it possible for them to love stone statues? But stone statues are comfortable. They don't create any trouble. You can do anything you want: you can pour water over them or milk over them, you can offer them rotten coconuts, and they will not even object. You can say anything in any language, right or wrong, to the stone statue, it does not matter.

Love needs the other to be living, alive. But then you have to learn the art. It is one of the stupidities that no university in the world teaches people the art of living, the art of loving, the art of meditating. And I think anything else is far lower than love, life, meditation, laughter. You may be a great surgeon, you may be a great engineer, you may be a great scientist – still you will need a sense of humor, still you will need the art of love, still you will need the art of living, still you will need all these great values in your life.

But you will be surprised. I teach only these things: love, life, laughter, and as a background for all these, meditation, but the government of India is not willing to accept this school as an institution of education. They would accept it as an institution of education if I were teaching geography, history, chemistry, physics – the mundane things of life.

I don't say that they should not be taught, but they should not be the only education. They should be a lower kind of education, and each university should have a higher faculty of education where you are taught real values of life because geography cannot make you a better man, nor can history make you a better lover, nor can chemistry make you meditative.

All that is being taught in the universities cannot give you a sense of humor. You cannot laugh, you cannot dance, you cannot sing. Your life becomes almost like a desert.

Zarathustra would like your life to be a garden where birds sing, where flowers blossom, where trees dance, where the sun comes with joy. Zarathustra is absolutely for life, and that is the reason why he does not have many followers. The poisoners, the destructive people, have millions of followers. And a unique teacher and a unique mystic whose whole message is love and life, has got the smallest religion in the world.

Zarathustra's religion should be the only religion. All other religions should be buried in the cemeteries because except for life there is no God, and except for love there is no prayer.

...Thus spake Zarathustra.

the camel, the lion, and the child

Of the Three Metamorphoses

I name you three metamorphoses of the spirit: how the spirit shall become a camel, and the camel a lion, and the lion at last a child.

There are many heavy things for the spirit, for the strong, weight-bearing spirit in which dwell respect and awe: its strength longs for the heavy, for the heaviest.

What is heavy? Thus asks the weight-bearing spirit, thus it kneels down like the camel and wants to be well laden.

What is the heaviest thing, you heroes? So asks the weight-bearing spirit, that I may take it upon me and rejoice in my strength.

Is it not this: to debase yourself in order to injure your pride?

Or is it this: to desert our cause when it is celebrating its victory? To climb high mountains in order to tempt the tempter?

Or is it this: to love those who despise us and to offer our hand to the ghost when it wants to frighten us?

The weight-bearing spirit takes upon itself all these heaviest things: like a camel hurrying laden into the desert, thus it hurries into its desert.

But in the loneliest desert the second metamorphosis occurs: the spirit here becomes a lion; it wants to capture freedom and be lord in its own desert.

It seeks here its ultimate lord: it will be an enemy to him and to its
ultimate God, it will struggle for victory with the great dragon.
What is the great dragon which the spirit no longer wants to call
lord and God? The great dragon is called "Thou shalt." But the
spirit of the lion says "I will!"
"Thou shalt" lies in its path, sparkling with gold, a scale-covered
beast, and on every scale glitters golden "Thou shalt."
Values of a thousand years glitter on the scales, and thus speaks the
mightiest of all dragons: "All the values of things – glitter on me.
"All values have already been created, and all created values – are in
me. Truly, there shall be no more 'I will'!" Thus speaks the dragon.
My brothers, why is the lion needed in the spirit? Why does the
beast of burden, that renounces and is reverent, not suffice?
To create new values – even the lion is incapable of that: but to
create itself freedom for new creation – that the might of the lion
can do.
To create freedom for itself and a sacred No even to duty: the lion is
needed for that, my brothers.
To seize the right to new values – that is the most terrible
proceeding for a weight-bearing and reverential spirit....
Once it loved this "Thou shalt" as its holiest thing: now it has to
find illusion and caprice even in the holiest, that it may steal
freedom from its love: the lion is needed for this theft.
But tell me, my brothers, what can the child do that even the lion
cannot? Why must the preying lion still become a child?
The child is innocence and forgetfulness, a new beginning, a sport,
a self-propelling wheel, a first motion, a sacred Yes.
Yes, a sacred Yes is needed, my brothers, for the sport of creation:
the spirit now wills its own will, the spirit sundered from the world
now wins its own world.
I have named you three metamorphoses of the spirit: how the spirit
became a camel, and the camel a lion, and the lion at last a child.

...Thus spake Zarathustra.

Zarathustra divides the evolution of consciousness into three
symbols: the camel, the lion, and the child.

The camel is a beast of burden, ready to be enslaved, never
rebellious. He cannot ever say no. He is a believer, a follower, a

faithful slave. That is the lowest in human consciousness.

The lion is a revolution. The beginning of the revolution is a sacred no.

In the consciousness of the camel there is always a need for someone to lead and someone to say to him, "Thou shalt do this." He needs the Ten Commandments. He needs all the religions, all the priests and all the holy scriptures because he cannot trust himself. He has no courage and no soul and no longing for freedom. He's obedient.

The lion is a longing for freedom, a desire to destroy all imprisonments. The lion is not in need of any leader; he is enough unto himself. He will not allow anybody else to say to him, "Thou shalt" – that is insulting to his pride. He can only say, "I will." The lion is responsibility, and a tremendous effort to get out of all chains.

But even the lion is not the highest peak of human growth. The highest peak is when the lion also goes through a metamorphosis and becomes a child. The child is innocence. It is not obedience, it is not disobedience; it is not belief, it is not disbelief – it is pure trust, it is a sacred yes to existence and to life and to all that it contains.

The child is the very peak of purity, sincerity, authenticity, receptivity, and openness to existence. These symbols are very beautiful.

We will go into the implications of these symbols as Zarathustra describes them, one by one.

> *I name you three metamorphoses of the spirit: how the spirit shall become a camel, and the camel a lion, and the lion at last a child. There are many heavy things for the spirit, for the strong, weight-bearing spirit in which dwell respect and awe: its strength longs for the heavy, for the heaviest.*

Zarathustra is not in favor of the weak, in favor of the so-called humble. He is not in agreement with Jesus: "Blessed are the meek," "Blessed are the poor," "Blessed are the humble for they shall inherit the kingdom of God."

Zarathustra is absolutely in favor of a strong spirit. He is against the ego, but he is not against pride. Pride is the dignity of man. Ego is a false entity and one should never think of them as synonymous.

The ego is something that deprives you of your dignity, that deprives you of your pride because the ego has to depend on others, on the opinion of others, on what people say. The ego is very fragile. The opinion of people can change and the ego will disappear into the air.

I am reminded of a great thinker, Voltaire...

In the days of Voltaire, in France, it was customary – a long, long tradition – that if you can get anything from a genius, just a piece of cloth, it will help you to find your own talents, if not to make you a genius yourself.

Voltaire was honored and respected so much as a great thinker and philosopher that he needed police protection even for his morning walk. If he was going to the railway station, police protection was needed. The police protection was needed because people would crowd around and start tearing his clothes. There were times he reached home almost naked, with scratches on his body, blood oozing, and he was very disturbed by the fame and the great name.

He wrote in his diary, "I used to think to be famous is something great, now I know it is a curse. And somehow I want again to be ordinary, anonymous; that nobody recognizes me, that I can pass by and nobody will take any note of me. I am tired of being famous, of being a celebrity. I have become a prisoner in my house. I cannot even go for a walk when the sky is so colorful and the sunset is so beautiful. I am afraid of the crowd."

The same crowd has made him a great man.

After ten years, in his diary he notes with great depression and sadness: "I was not aware that my prayers would be heard." Fashions change, people's opinions change. Somebody is famous today, tomorrow nobody remembers him. Somebody is not known today, and tomorrow suddenly rises to the heights of fame.

And it happened in the case of Voltaire. Slowly, slowly new thinkers, new philosophers arrived on the horizon. Rousseau particularly took the place where Voltaire used to be once, and people forgot about Voltaire. People's memories are not very reliable.

Opinions change just like fashions. Once he was fashionable, now somebody else has become fashionable. Rousseau was against every idea of Voltaire; his fame destroyed Voltaire completely. Voltaire's prayer was fulfilled; he became anonymous. Now, no police protection was needed. Now, nobody even bothered to say "hello" to him. People had completely forgotten. Only then he realized that to be a prisoner was better. "Now I am free to move anywhere, but it hurts. The wound goes on becoming bigger and bigger – I am alive and it seems that people have thought Voltaire is dead."

When he died, only three and a half people followed him to the graveyard. You will be surprised, why three and a half? – because three were people, and his dog can be counted only as half. The dog was leading the procession.

Ego is a by-product of public opinion. It is given by the public to you; they can take it away. Pride is a totally different phenomenon. The lion has pride. Just look, the deer in the forest has a pride, a dignity, a grace. A peacock dancing or an eagle flying far away in the sky – they don't have egos, they don't depend on your opinion; they are simply dignified as they are. Their dignity arises from their own being. This has to be understood because all the religions have been teaching people not to be proud – be humble. They have created a misunderstanding all over the world, as if being proud and being an egoist are synonymous.

Zarathustra is absolutely clear that he is in favor of the strong man, of the courageous man, of the adventurer who goes into the unknown on the untrodden path without any fear. He is in favor of fearlessness. And it is a miracle that a man of pride, and only a man of pride, can become a child.

The so-called Christian humbleness is just ego standing on its head. The ego has gone upside down, but it is there, and you can see in your saints that they are more egoist than ordinary people are. They are egoists because of their piousness, of their austerities, of their spirituality, of their holiness, even of their humbleness. Nobody is more humble than them. The ego has a very subtle way of coming in from the back door. You may throw it out from the front door – it knows that there is a back door too.

I have heard that one night, in a pub, a man was drinking too much and making a nuisance: throwing things, hitting people, shouting, abusing them and asking for more and more drinks.

Finally, the pub owner told him, "This is enough. For tonight, you will not get any more drinks." And he told his servants to throw him out of the front door.

Although he was completely drunk, even in his drunkenness he remembered there was a back door. Groping in the dark, he came from the back door and ordered a drink.

The owner said, "Again? I have told you that tonight you will not get any drink."

The man said, "This is strange. Do you own all the pubs of the city?"

The ego knows not only the back door, it can come in even through the windows. It can come in even by removing a small tile from the roof. You are so vulnerable as far as the ego is concerned.

Zarathustra is not a teacher of humbleness because all teachings of humbleness have failed. He teaches the dignity of man. He teaches the pride of man and he teaches the strong man, not the weak, the poor and the meek. Those teachings have helped to keep humanity at the stage of the camel. Zarathustra wants you to go through a metamorphosis. The camel has to change into a lion, and he has chosen beautiful symbols, very meaningful and significant.

The camel is perhaps the ugliest animal in the whole existence. You cannot improve upon its ugliness. What else can you do? It is such a distortion. It seems as if it is coming directly from hell.

To choose the camel as the lowest consciousness is perfectly right. The lowest consciousness in man is crippled; it wants to be enslaved. It is afraid of freedom because it is afraid of responsibility. The camel is ready to be loaded with as much burden as possible. It rejoices in being loaded; so does the lowest consciousness – being loaded with knowledge, which is borrowed. No man of dignity will allow himself to be loaded with borrowed knowledge. It is loaded with morality, which has been handed over by the dead to the living. It is a domination of the dead over the living. No man of dignity will allow the dead to rule him.

The lowest consciousness of man remains ignorant and unconscious, unaware, fast asleep because it is continuously being given the poison of belief, of faith, of never doubting, of never saying no. And a man who cannot say no has lost his dignity. And a man who cannot say no – his yes does not mean anything. Do you see the implication? The yes is meaningful only after you are capable of saying no. If you are incapable of saying no, your yes is impotent, it means nothing.

Hence, the camel has to change into a beautiful lion, ready to die but not ready to be enslaved. You cannot make a lion a beast of burden. A lion has a dignity that no other animal can claim; he has no treasures, no kingdoms. His dignity is just in his style of being – fearless, unafraid of the unknown, ready to say no even at the risk of death.

This readiness to say no, this rebelliousness, cleans him of all the dirt that the camel has left – all the traces and the footprints that the camel has left. And only after the lion, after the great no, is the sacred yes of a child possible.

The child says yes not because he is afraid. He says yes because he loves, because he trusts. He says yes because he is innocent; he cannot conceive that he can be deceived. His yes is a tremendous trust. It is not out of fear, it is out of deep innocence. Only this yes can lead him to the ultimate peak of consciousness; what I call godliness.

> There are many heavy things for the spirit, for the strong, weight-bearing spirit in which dwell respect and awe: its strength longs for the heavy, for the heaviest.
> What is heavy? Thus asks the weight-bearing spirit, thus it kneels down like the camel and wants to be well laden.

For the camel, for the lowest kind of consciousness, there is an intrinsic desire to kneel down and to be laden with as much load as possible.

> What is the heaviest thing, you heroes? So asks the weight-bearing spirit, that I may take it upon me and rejoice in my strength.

But to the strong man, to the lion in you, the heaviest takes on a different meaning and a different dimension: ...that I may take it upon me and rejoice in my strength. Its only joy is its strength. The camel's joy is only to be obedient, to serve, to be a slave.

> Is it not this: to debase yourself in order to injure your pride?
> Or is it this: to desert our cause when it is celebrating its victory? To climb high mountains in order to tempt the tempter?
> Or is it this: to love those who despise us and to offer our hand to the ghost when it wants to frighten us?

*The weight-bearing spirit takes upon itself all these heaviest things: like
a camel hurrying laden into the desert, thus it hurries into its desert.*

The lowest consciousness of man knows only a life of the desert:
where nothing grows, where nothing is green, where no flower blos-
soms, where everything is dead and, as far as you can see, it is a
vast graveyard.

*But in the loneliest desert the second metamorphosis occurs: the
spirit here becomes a lion...*

There are moments, even in the life of those who are groping in
darkness and unconsciousness, when just like lightning, some incident wakes them up and the camel is no longer a camel: a metamorphosis, a transformation happens.

Gautam Buddha left his kingdom when he was twenty-nine years
old and the reason: a sudden lightning and the camel became a lion.

When he was born, all the great astrologers of the kingdom were
called because he was the only son of the great emperor, and he was
born when the emperor was getting old. It was his lifelong prayer,
lifelong desire to have a child; otherwise, who was going to succeed
him? His whole life he had been fighting, invading and creating a vast
empire. For whom? There was great rejoicing when Gautam Buddha
was born and he wanted to know, in detail, the future of the child. All
the great astrologers assembled in the palace. They discussed for
hours and the king asked again and again, "What is your conclusion?
Why is it taking so long?"

Finally, the youngest – because all the old ones were feeling very
embarrassed. "What to say?" The situation was such, they were all
in agreement. But the youngest stood up and he said, "These are old
people and they don't want to say anything that may hurt you. But
somebody has to break the ice.

"You have a very strange child. His future cannot be predicted
definitely because he has two futures. For hours we have been discussing which one is heavier; they both are of equal weight. We have
never come across such a child."

The king said, "Don't be worried. Tell me exactly, but tell me
the truth."

And the astrologer said, with everybody's agreement, "Either your child will become the greatest emperor the world has ever known, a *chakravartin*, or he will renounce the kingdom and will become a beggar. That's why we were delaying, and we could not find the right words to tell you this. Both possibilities have equal weight."

The king was very much puzzled and he asked, "Can you advise me? Is there some way that he does not renounce the world and become a beggar?" They suggested all kinds of measures; particularly, that he should not become aware of sickness, old age, death, sannyasins. He should be kept in such a way – almost blind to these realities because anything can trigger the idea of renouncing the world. The king said, "Don't be worried. That much care I can take."

Three great palaces were made for him for different seasons, so he never felt the heat or the cold or too much rain. All kinds of comforts were arranged. The gardeners were ordered: "He should not be allowed to see a dead leaf, a flower that is withering away, so in the night, clean the garden completely of all old flowers, old leaves. He should remain only aware of youth, of young flowers." He was surrounded by all the beautiful girls of the kingdom as he came of age. His whole time was nothing but pleasure, entertainment, music, dancing, beautiful women – and he had not seen anybody sick.

It was at the age of twenty-nine that there used to be an annual affair, a kind of youth festival, and the prince had to inaugurate it. He had been inaugurating it for years; roads were closed, people had to keep their old men and women behind doors. But this year... The story is very beautiful: up to now, it seems to be a historical thing. Beyond this point something of mythology enters into it, but the mythology is more important than the historical facts.

The story is, that the gods in heaven... You must be made aware that Jainism and Buddhism don't believe in one god, they believe that every being is going to be a god, finally. Zarathustra will agree with them: to be a god is everybody's potential. How long he takes depends on him, but that is his destiny. And millions of people have reached that point; they don't have physical bodies, they live in eternity, in immortality.

The gods in heaven became very disturbed that almost twenty-nine years have passed; a man who is supposed to be a great, enlightened being is being prevented by his father. To be a great emperor is meaningless in comparison to becoming the greatest awakened man

in history because that will raise the consciousness of humanity and
the whole universe.

I say this is non-historical but mythology is more significant
because it shows that the whole existence is interested in your growth,
that existence is not indifferent to you. And if you are very close to
blossoming, existence will be ready to bring your spring as soon as
possible. Existence has a vested interest in your becoming awakened
because your awakening is going to awaken many people.

And as a general rule, the whole consciousness of humanity will
be affected by it. It will leave its imprint of grandeur on every intelligent human being. Perhaps it may create the longing for the same in
many; perhaps the seed may start sprouting. Perhaps that which is
dormant will become active, dynamic.

That's why I say this mythological part is far more significant
than the historical facts. It may be pure story, but it is tremendously
symbolic.

The roads were closed, so the gods decided that one god would
appear first as a sick man, coughing, by the side of the golden
chariot in which Gautam Buddha was going to inaugurate the annual
youth festival. Buddha could not believe what had happened to this
man. So much care had been taken of him; the greatest physicians
of the day had been taking care of him and he had not known any
disease. He had not known anyone around him to be sick.

Another of the gods entered the charioteer, because Buddha
asked the charioteer, "What has happened to this man?"

The god answered from the charioteer's mouth: "This happens
to everybody. Sooner or later, man starts becoming weak, sick, old."
When he was saying this they saw an old man – another god – and
the charioteer said, "Look, that is what happens to everybody. Youth
is not eternal. It is ephemeral."

Buddha was very shocked. Just then they saw a third party of
gods carrying a dead man, a corpse, going to the funeral grounds,
and Buddha said, "What has happened to this man?"

And the charioteer said, "After old age, this is the end. The curtain falls. This man is dead."

Just behind that procession was coming a red-robed sannyasin
and Buddha asked, "Why is this man wearing red clothes, shaven
head? He looks very joyous, very healthy, has a shine in his eyes
and a certain magnetism. Who is he? What has happened to him?"

The charioteer said, "This man, seeing sickness, disease, old age, death, renounced the world. Before death comes, he wants to know the truth of life – whether life is going to survive after death or death is all, and everything finishes. He is a seeker of truth. He is a sannyasin."

This was like lightning. Twenty-nine years of his father's efforts simply disappeared. He told the charioteer, "I am not going to inaugurate the youth festival because where disease happens and death happens, what is the point of being young for a few years? Somebody else can do it. You turn back." And that very night, he escaped from the palace in search of truth.

The camel has changed into a lion. The metamorphosis has happened. Anything can trigger it, but one needs intelligence.

But in the loneliest desert the second metamorphosis occurs: the spirit here becomes a lion; it wants to capture freedom and be lord in its own desert.
It seeks here its ultimate lord: it will be an enemy to him and to its ultimate God...

Now his search is for his ultimate godliness. Any other god will be an enemy to him. He is not going to bow down to any other god, he is going to be a lord unto himself. That is the spirit of the lion – absolute freedom certainly means freedom from God, freedom from so-called commandments, freedom from scriptures, freedom from any kind of morality imposed by others.

Certainly, there will arise a virtue, but that will be something coming from your own still, small voice. Your freedom will bring responsibility, but that responsibility will not be imposed on you by anyone else:

...it will struggle for victory with the great dragon.
What is the great dragon which the spirit no longer wants to call lord and God? The great dragon is called "Thou shalt." But the spirit of the lion says "I will!"

Now, there is no question of anybody else ordering him. Even God is no longer anybody he has to obey.

Zarathustra, somewhere, has a great statement: "God is dead

and man is for the first time free." With God being there, man can never be free. He can be politically free, he can be economically free, he can be socially free, but spiritually, he will remain a slave and he will remain just a puppet.

The very idea that God created man destroys all possibility of freedom. If he has created you, he can uncreate you. He has put you together, he can take you apart. If he is the creator, he has every possibility and potentiality to be a destroyer.

You cannot prevent him. You could not prevent him from creating you, how can you prevent him from destroying you? It is because of this that Gautam Buddha, Mahavira and Zarathustra, three great seers of the world, have denied the existence of God.

You will be surprised. Their argument for denying God is a very strange argument, but very significant. They say, "While God is there, man has no possibility of becoming totally free."

Man's freedom, his spiritual dignity, depends on there being no God. If God is there, then man will remain a camel, worshipping dead statues, worshipping somebody he has not known, somebody who has never been known by anybody – just a pure hypothesis. You are worshipping a hypothesis. All your temples and churches and synagogues are nothing but monuments raised in honor of a hypothesis which is absolutely unproved, without any evidence. There exists no argument for God's existence as a person who created the world.

Zarathustra uses very strong language. He is a man of strong language. All authentic men have always been of strong language. He calls God, "the great dragon." *What is the great dragon which the spirit no longer wants to call lord and God? The great dragon is called "Thou shalt."*

All religious scriptures are included in these two words: *Thou shalt.* You should do this and you should not do this. You are not free to choose what is right. It has been decided by people who have been dead for thousands of years what is right and what is wrong for all the coming future.

A man who has a rebellious spirit – and without a rebellious spirit, the metamorphosis cannot happen – has to say: "No, I will. I will do whatever my consciousness feels to be right, and I will not do whatever my consciousness feels to be wrong. Except my own being, there is no other guide for me. Except my own eyes, I am not going to believe in anyone else's eyes. I am not blind, and I am not an idiot.

"I can see. I can think. I can meditate and I can find out for myself what is right and what is wrong. My morality will be simply the shadow of my consciousness."

"Thou shalt" lies in its path, sparkling with gold, a scale-covered beast, and on every scale glitters golden "Thou shalt."
Values of a thousand years glitter on the scales, and thus speaks the mightiest of all dragons: "All the values of things – glitter on me.
"All values have already been created, and all created values – are in me. Truly, there shall be no more 'I will'!" Thus speaks the dragon.

All the religions, all the religious heads are included in the dragon. They all say that all values have been created, that there is no need for you to decide anymore. Everything has been decided for you by wiser people than you. There is no need of "I will."

But without "I will" there is no freedom. You remain a camel, and that's what all the vested interests: religious, political and social, want you to be – just camels; ugly, without any dignity, without any grace, without any soul, just ready to serve, very willing to be slaves. The very idea of freedom has not happened to them. And these are not philosophical statements. These are truths.

Has the idea of freedom ever happened to the Hindus, or the Christians, or the Buddhists, or the Mohammedans? No. They all say with one voice: "Everything has been decided already. We have simply to follow. And those who follow are virtuous and those who don't follow will fall into the hellfire for eternity."

My brothers, why is the lion needed in the spirit? Why does the beast of burden, that renounces and is reverent, not suffice?

Zarathustra is saying that your so-called saints are nothing but perfect camels. They have said yes to the dead traditions, dead conventions, dead scriptures, dead gods, and because they are perfect camels, imperfect camels worship them – naturally.

To create new values – even the lion is incapable of that: but to create itself freedom for new creation – that the might of the lion can do.

The lion cannot create himself new values but he can create the freedom, the opportunity in which new values can be created. And what are the new values?

For example, the new man cannot believe in any discrimination amongst human beings. That will be a new value: all human beings are one, in spite of their color, in spite of their race, in spite of their geographies, in spite of their histories. Just being human is enough.

The new value should be: there should be no nations at all because they have been the cause of all wars.

There should be no organized religions because they have been preventing individual search. They go on handing over to people ready-made truths, and truth is not a toy, you cannot get it ready-made. There is no factory that manufactures it and there is no market where it is available. You will have to search for it in the deepest silences of your own heart. And except you, nobody else can go there. Religion is individual – this is a new value.

Nations are ugly, religious organizations are irreligious, churches and temples and synagogues and *gurudwaras* are just ridiculous. The whole of existence is sacred. The whole of existence is the temple. And wherever you sit silently, meditatively, lovingly, you create a temple of consciousness around you. You need not go anywhere to worship because there is nobody higher than your consciousness to whom you owe any worship.

To create freedom for itself and a sacred No even to duty: the lion is needed for that, my brothers.

You have been told continually that duty is a great value. In fact, it is a four-letter…a dirty word. If you love your wife because it is your duty, then you don't love. You love your duty, you don't love your wife. If you love your mother because it is your duty, you don't love your mother. Duty destroys all that is beautiful in man – love, compassion, joy. People even laugh because it is their duty.

I have heard that in one office the boss used to call all the people, just before the office day began, into his room. He knew only three jokes, and every day he would tell a joke, and it was, of course, absolutely necessary that everybody laughed. It was a duty. And they were bored with those jokes because they had heard them thousands of times, but still they would laugh as if they were hearing it for the first time. One day, when he told the joke, everybody laughed – only a girl who was a typist did not laugh.

The boss said, "What is the matter with you? Did you hear the joke or not?"

She said, "The joke? I am resigning from this post. I have joined another office. Now it is no longer a duty for me to laugh at a joke that I have heard at least ten thousand times. Let all these idiots laugh because these poor fellows still have to remain in this office."

Teachers want students to respect them because it is their duty. I was a professor and the education commission of India invited a few professors from all over India to participate in a conference in New Delhi on important issues which were becoming more and more troublesome in every educational institute.

The first was: students don't pay any respect to the professors. Many professors spoke on it, saying, "Something has to be done urgently because unless there is respect, the whole educational system will fall apart."

I could not understand what kind of discussion this was because not a single person had objected or argued on the point. I was the youngest person and I was called because the chairman of the education committee, D. S. Kothari, had heard me while he was visiting a university. He was one of the prominent scientists of India. I was very junior and it was a conference of old, senior people.

But I said, "It seems I have to speak on this subject because all these professors are insisting on one thing, that every student has a duty to be respectful toward the teacher, and none of them has said that the teacher has to be deserving of respect. My own experience in the university is that not a single professor is worthy of any respect. And if students are not being respectful, to impose it as a duty will be absolutely ugly and fascist. I am against it. I would like the commission to decide that teachers should be worthy and deserving, and respect will follow automatically.

"Whenever there is someone who is beautiful, people's eyes immediately recognize the beauty. Whenever there is someone who has some character, some dignity, people simply respect. It is not a question of demanding or making it a rule that every student should respect.

"The university is not part of your army. The university should teach every student to be free, to be alert, to be conscious. And the whole burden is on the professors to prove themselves worthy of it."

They were all angry with me. D. S. Kothari told me after the conference, "They were very angry with you and they were asking me, 'Why did you call him, knowing perfectly well that he cannot agree on any point with anybody and anyway, he is so junior and this is a conference of senior professors.'"

I told D. S. Kothari, "They are senior professors, but not a single one of them was able to answer the question that I had raised, 'Why should you hanker for respect?' In fact, only people who don't deserve respect desire that they should be respected. People who deserve respect get it. It is simply natural. But to make it a duty is ugly."

Zarathustra is right:

To create freedom for itself and a sacred No even to duty: the lion is needed for that...
To seize the right to new values – that is the most terrible proceeding for a weight-bearing and reverential spirit....
Once it loved this "Thou shalt" as its holiest thing: now it has to find illusion and caprice even in the holiest, that it may steal freedom from its love: the lion is needed for this theft.
But tell me, my brothers, what can the child do that even the lion cannot? Why must the preying lion still become a child?
The child is innocence and forgetfulness, a new beginning, a sport, a self-propelling wheel, a first motion, a sacred Yes.
Yes, a sacred Yes is needed, my brothers, for the sport of creation: the spirit now wills its own will, the spirit sundered from the world now wins its own world.
I have named you three metamorphoses of the spirit: how the spirit became a camel, and the camel a lion, and the lion at last a child.

The child is the highest peak of evolution as far as consciousness is concerned. But the child is only a symbol; it does not mean that children are the highest state of being. A child is used symbolically because it is not knowledgeable. It is innocent, and because it is innocent it is full of wonder, and because its eyes are full of wonder, its soul longs for the mysterious. A child is a beginning, a

sport; and life should always be a beginning and always a playfulness; always a laughter and never seriousness.

...*a first motion, a sacred Yes.* Yes, a sacred yes is needed, but
the sacred yes can come only after a sacred no. The camel also
says yes but it is the yes of a slave. He cannot say no. His yes is
meaningless.

The lion says no! But he cannot say yes. It is against his very
nature. It reminds him of the camel. Somehow he has freed himself
from the camel and to say yes naturally reminds him of the yes of
the camel and the slavery. No, the animal in the camel is incapable
of saying no. In the lion, it is capable of saying no but is incapable of
saying yes.

The child knows nothing of the camel, knows nothing of the lion.
That's why Zarathustra says: ...*the child is innocence and forgetfulness*... His yes is pure and he has every potential to say no. If he
does not say it, it is because he trusts, not because he is afraid; not
out of fear, but out of trust. And when yes comes out of trust, it is the
greatest metamorphosis, the greatest transformation that one can
hope for.

These three symbols are beautiful to remember. Remember that
you are where the camel is, and remember that you have to move
toward the lion, and remember that you have not to stop at the lion.
You have to move even further, to a new beginning, to innocence
and to a sacred yes; to a child.

The real sage again becomes a child.

The circle is complete – from the child back to the child. But
the difference is great. The child, as such, is ignorant. He will have
to pass through the camel, through the lion, and come back again to
the child. And this child is not exactly the old child because it is not
ignorant. It has moved through all the experiences of life: of slavery,
of freedom, of an impotent yes, of a ferocious no, and yet it has forgotten all that. It is not ignorance but innocence. The first child was
the beginning of a journey. The second childhood is the completion
of the journey.

In India, in the days when Zarathustra was writing these statements
in Iran, the Upanishads were being written, which have the same
understanding. In the Upanishads, the brahmin is one who comes
to know the ultimate reality. Not by birth is anybody a brahmin, but
only by knowing the *brahman*, the ultimate reality, one becomes a

brahmin. And another name of brahmin in the Upanishads is *dwij*, twice born. The first birth is of the body and the second birth is of the consciousness.

The first birth makes you human, the second birth makes you a god.

...Thus spake Zarathustra.

love is the dance of your life

Of Life and Love

What have we in common with the rosebud, which trembles because a drop of dew is lying upon it?

It is true: we love life, not because we are used to living but because we are used to loving.

There is always a certain madness in love. But also there is always a certain method in madness.

And to me too, who love life, it seems that butterflies and soap bubbles, and whatever is like them among men, know most about happiness.

To see these light, foolish, dainty, affecting little souls flutter about – that moves Zarathustra to tears and to song.

I should believe only in a God who understood how to dance.

Of War and Warriors

We do not wish to be spared by our best enemies, nor by those whom we love from the very heart. So let me tell you the truth! My brothers in war! I love you from the very heart, I am and have always been of your kind. And I am also your best enemy. So let me tell you the truth!...

You should be such men as are always looking for an enemy – for your enemy. And with some of you there is hate at first sight.
You should seek your enemy, you should wage your war – a war for your opinions. And if your opinion is defeated, your honesty should still cry triumph over that!
You should love peace as a means to new wars. And the short peace more than the long.
I do not exhort you to work but to battle. I do not exhort you to peace, but to victory. May your work be a battle, may your peace be a victory!
One can be silent and sit still only when one has arrow and bow; otherwise one babbles and quarrels. May your peace be a victory!
You say it is the good cause that hallows even war? I tell you: it is the good war that hallows every cause.
War and courage have done more great things than charity. Not your pity but your bravery has saved the unfortunate up to now....
Thus live your life of obedience and war! What good is long life? What warrior wants to be spared?

...Thus spake Zarathustra.

Z arathustra is a lover of life, and without any conditions. His approach to life is unique to himself and because it is so unique it has to be understood very silently, without any prejudice. He is speaking against all your prejudices, he is speaking against all your religions, he is speaking against all the values that you have thought are great.

When somebody speaks against everything that you have believed in, your mind stops listening; it becomes afraid, it closes, it becomes defensive. It is afraid – perhaps you have been wrong, and perhaps the man who is speaking against you may be right. It hurts your ego.

So the first thing I want to say to you is: put your prejudices aside. That does not mean that you have to agree with Zarathustra; that simply means, before any agreement or disagreement, give him a chance to make his standpoint clear to you. Then it is your freedom to accept him or not to accept him.

My own experience is that if you can listen to him silently, you will be amazed that although he is speaking against all your traditions, all your conventions, all your so-called great teachers, still he has some tremendous truth in whatever he is saying. And that truth will be revealed in your silence, without any difficulty.

Once you have listened to him, it is almost impossible to disagree with him because he is saying the truth, although the truth goes against the beliefs of the crowd. Truth always goes against the beliefs of the crowd.

The truth is individual, and the crowd does not care about truth. It cares about consolation; it cares about comfort. The crowd does not consist of explorers, adventurers, people who go into the unknown, fearless – risking their whole lives to find the meaning and the significance of their lives, and the life of the whole of existence. The crowd simply wants to be told things which are sweet to hear, comfortable and cozy; without any effort on their part, they can relax in those consoling lies.

It happened...

The last time I went to my hometown was in 1970. One of my old teachers, with whom I always had a very loving relationship, was on his deathbed. So the first thing I did was to go to his house.

His son met me at the door and told me, "Please, don't disturb him. He is just on the verge of death. He loves you, he has been remembering you, but we know that your very presence may take away his consolations. And at the moment of death, do not do this to him."

I said, "If it was not the moment of death I would have listened to your advice – I have to see him. Even if before he dies he drops his lies and consolations, his death will have a value even greater than his life had."

I pushed the son aside. I went in the house. The old man opened his eyes, smiled, and he said, "I was remembering you and at the same time I was afraid. I heard that you were coming to the town, and thought that perhaps before I die, I might be able to see you one time more. But at the same time there was great fear, as meeting with you can be dangerous!"

I said, "It is certainly going to be dangerous. I have come at the right time. I want to take away all your consolations before you die. If you can die innocent, your death will have a tremendous value. Put aside your knowledge because it is all borrowed. Put aside your

God because it is only a belief, and nothing more. Put aside the idea of any heaven or hell because they are only your greed and your fear. Your whole life, you have remained clinging to these things. At least before you die, gather courage – now you have nothing to lose!

"A dying man cannot lose anything: death is going to shatter everything. It is better you drop your consolations by your own hand and die innocently, full of wonder and inquiry because death is the ultimate experience in life. It is the very crescendo."

The old man said, "I was afraid, and now you are asking me the same thing. I have worshipped God my whole life, and I know it is only a hypothesis – I have never experienced it. I have prayed to the skies, and I know no prayer has ever been replied – there is no one to reply to it. But it has been consolatory in the sufferings of life, in the anxieties of life. What else can a helpless man do?"

I said, "Now you are no longer helpless, now there is no question of any anxiety, no suffering, no problems; they belong to life. Now life has slipped out of your hands, maybe a few minutes longer you will linger here on this shore. Gather courage! Don't encounter death as a coward."

He closed his eyes, and he said, "I will try my best."

His whole family gathered; they were all angry with me. They were high-caste brahmins, very orthodox, and they could not believe that the old man had agreed with me. Death was such a shock that it shattered all his lies.

In life you can go on believing in lies, but in death you know perfectly well that boats made of paper are not going to help in the ocean. It is better to know that you have to swim, and you don't have any boat. Clinging to a paper boat is dangerous; it may prevent you from swimming. Rather than taking you to the further shore, it may become the cause of your drowning.

They were all angry but they could not say anything. And, with closed eyes the old man smiled and said, "It is unfortunate that I never listened to you. I am feeling so light, so unburdened. I am feeling so fearless; not only fearless but curious to die and to see what is the mystery of death."

He died, and the smile remained on his face. He died not as a camel; he died as a child.

Within those few moments, all the steps from camel to the lion, from lion to the child happened so quickly. It was not a question of time.

The metamorphosis of which Zarathustra is speaking is a question of intense understanding.

Listen to his words because these are not ordinary words: these are the words of a man who knows life from its very roots, and of a man who is uncompromising, of a man who will not accept any lie, howsoever comfortable, howsoever consolatory it may be.

These words are the words of a soul which knows freedom. These words are like the roar of a lion. These words are also the stammering of a child, utterly innocent. These words are not out of knowledge, they are not coming from the head – they are coming directly from his being.

If you can listen to them in silence and with deep sympathy, falling into a kind of rapport, only then is there a possibility to understand this strange man, Zarathustra.

It is easy to understand Jesus, it is easy to understand Gautam Buddha; it is far more difficult to understand Zarathustra because nobody has spoken like him. Nobody could have spoken like him because they were all in search of followers.

He was not in search of followers. He was in search of companions, of friends, of fellow travelers. He was not in search of believers: he will not say something just so that it appeals to you, just so that it fits with your prejudiced mind. He will say only that which is true to his experience. Even if nobody agrees with him, even if he has to go alone, and he finds no companions and no fellow travelers, still, he is going to say only the truth, and nothing but truth.

What have we in common with the rosebud, which trembles because a drop of dew is lying upon it?

Have you seen in the early morning sun, a rosebud with a dewdrop shining with the soft rays of the sun, almost like a pearl – and the rosebud is dancing in the wind?

He is asking: *What have we in common with the rosebud, which trembles because a drop of dew is lying upon it?* There is no meaning, no purpose, in the sense that *purpose* is understood in the marketplace. But the rosebud is immensely joyful – the dewdrop and the rising sun and the morning breeze. The moment is precious; it is a moment of dance.

This dance is not going to bring money, this dance is not going to bring fame, this dance is not going to make the rosebud respectable. This dance is not for anybody else to see; it is not waiting for an audience to applaud. This dance is a value in itself; it is a joy, purposeless, meaningless. It is not a commodity.

That is what is common between us and the rosebud. We should also rejoice in the moment. We should also dance in the sun, in the wind, in the rain. And the dance in itself is the reward. You should not ask, "For what?" We have forgotten all intrinsic values and Zarathustra is reminding us that values are not outside us, they are intrinsic.

When I was a student in the university, I used to wake up early, three o'clock in the morning. The university was surrounded by mountains, and at three o'clock in the night the roads were empty, no traffic. I used to run for miles. Slowly, slowly students started asking, "What is the purpose of it?"

I said, "Purpose? It is so joyous to be in the wind, in the silent night full of stars, no traffic on the road; the trees are fast asleep on both sides of the road. It was a fairyland, and to dance with the wind..."

A few became interested, just out of curiosity, "One day at least, I am going to come." Slowly, slowly a group of almost two dozen students started dancing on those roads. The manager of the university canteen approached me and he said, "I will not take any money from you for your food, for your milk, for your tea – even for your guests. But stop what you have started! These twenty boys used to eat two, three chapatis at the most; now they are eating twenty chapatis. You will kill me, I am a poor contractor: now twenty boys are eating almost the food that was enough for two hundred students. Have mercy on me."

I said, "It will be very difficult for me to prevent them because they have tasted the joy."

But he said, "Something has to be done, otherwise I will go bankrupt. Think of my children, of my wife, of my old parents."

I said to him, "You come with me to the vice-chancellor because I cannot prevent them. In fact, their number is going to grow because they are spreading the news to everybody: 'We have been idiots, wasting the most significant time in sleeping; and dancing under the stars in the early morning breeze is so beautiful that we have never known any other experience so ecstatic. Health is just a by-product of it. We are feeling our intelligence become sharper, but that too is a by-product. We are not going for this morning dance in the dark to sharpen the intellect or to have a better body, a more athletic body.'"

I had to explain to the vice-chancellor that this poor contractor was in a difficulty, and he should take care that the budget that has been given to him will be enough; these twenty dancing students are not going to remain twenty!

The vice-chancellor said, "But this is going to be difficult. If you turn on the whole university, not only will this contractor go bankrupt, but the whole university will go bankrupt. Twenty chapatis each student!"

I said, "But what can I do?"

He asked, "But what is the purpose of it all?"

I said, "Come one day because it is a purposeless activity."

He said, "I am coming tomorrow."

And I told the contractor, "You also come."

And they both joined us, and they said, "My God, it is really beautiful. This silence, these stars, no traffic on the road, no fear of anybody watching you – you can just dance like a small child."

The vice-chancellor said to the contractor, "I will make arrangements. You will not go at a loss, don't be worried. I can understand that those who have tasted cannot be prevented."

Once in a while, the vice-chancellor used to join us. And when the vice-chancellor joined us and a few professors, it became prestigious.

I used to go, whenever it was raining, on a lonely street; and soon a few people started going with me, without any umbrella – just enjoying the rain.

The vice-chancellor said to me, "Now you are creating more trouble. Soon the man who takes care of the laundry will be here. From where do you get these ideas? The rain has been happening every year. I have been here for ten years, and nobody has gone into the rain before; and you are spreading the idea that going into the rain is such an ecstatic experience."

I said, "Come one day."

He said, "You are a great salesman! I am not going to come because I know you must be right."

But he came. I said, "What happened?"

He said, "I could not resist the temptation that perhaps I am missing something. My whole life I have never been just going under the rain, under the clouds, under the lightning."

He was old, but he enjoyed it so much. He hugged me, he took me to his home, and he said, "You are a little crazy, there is no doubt about it; but your ideas are significant. But please, don't spread this new idea in the university; otherwise, students will leave the classes, and go into the rain."

It was so beautiful because all around the university there were hills, tall trees, and no traffic at all. It was outside the city, and dancing with the rain and with the wind...

There is no reason for life. That's what is in common with the rosebud. Gautam Buddha will not say that; neither will Mahavira, nor Jesus, nor Moses. They will all give you reasons, goals, purposes, because that is what appeals to your mind.

It is true: we love life, not because we are used to living...

Not just as a habit:

...but because we are used to loving.

The emphasis has to be remembered *...we love life, not because we are used to living...* You cannot say, "I have been alive for seventy years, now it has become an old habit – that's why I go on living, that's why I want to continue living because to drop old habits is very difficult."

No, life is not a habit. You love life, not because you have become accustomed to living *...but because we are used to loving.*

Without life there would not be any love. Life is an opportunity: the soil where the roses of love blossom. Love in itself is valuable, it has no purpose, it has no meaning. It has immense significance, it has great joy, it has an ecstasy of its own; but those are not meanings. Love is not a business where purposes, goals, matter.

There is always a certain madness in love.

And what is that madness? The madness is because you cannot

prove why you love. You cannot give any reasonable answer for your love. You can say you do a certain business because you need money; you need money because you need a house; you need a house because how can you live without a house?

In your ordinary life, everything has some purpose, but love – you cannot give any reason. You can simply say, "I don't know. All I know is that to love is to experience the most beautiful space within oneself." But it is not a purpose. That space is not salable. That space cannot be converted into a commodity. That space is again a rosebud, with a dewdrop on top of it shining like a pearl. And in the early morning breeze and in the sun, the rosebud is dancing.

Love is the dance of your life.

Hence those who don't know what love is have missed the very dance of life; they have missed the opportunity to grow roses. That's why, to the worldly mind, to the calculative mind, to the computer mind, to the mathematician, to the economist, to the politician, love appears to be a kind of madness.

There is always a certain madness in love. But also there is always a certain method in madness.

This statement is so beautiful, so remarkable. Love appears to others, who have never experienced it, as madness. But to those who know love, love is the only sanity. Without love, a man may be rich, healthy, famous, but he cannot be sane because he does not know anything of intrinsic value. Sanity is nothing but the fragrance of roses blossoming in your heart. Zarathustra has a great insight when he says, "But this madness, the madness known as love, is always with a certain method, it is not ordinary madness."

Lovers don't need psychiatric treatment. Love has its own method. In fact, love is the greatest healing force in life. Those who have missed it have remained empty, unfulfilled. Ordinary madness has no method, but the madness called love has a certain method in it. And what is that method? It makes you joyous, it makes your life a song, it brings great grace to you.

Have you watched people? When somebody falls in love there is no need for him to declare it. You can see in his eyes a new depth has arisen. You can see in his face a new grace, a new beauty. You can see in his walk a subtle dance. He is the same man, yet he is not the same man. Love has entered his life, spring has come to his being, flowers within his soul have blossomed.

Love makes immediate transformations.

The man who cannot love cannot be intelligent either; cannot be graceful either; cannot be beautiful either. His life will simply be a tragedy.

And to me too, who love life, it seems that butterflies and soap bubbles, and whatever is like them among men, know most about happiness.

It will hit you hard if you don't put your prejudices aside because all the religious teachers have been telling you: "Your life is futile because it is nothing but a soap bubble. Today it is there, tomorrow it is gone. Your life in this world, in this body, is not of any worth because it is momentary. Its only use is that you can renounce it. And by renouncing it you can attain to virtue in the eyes of God."

A strange ideology! But for centuries it has been dominating the human mind without ever being challenged. Particularly in the East, the world is illusory, and why is it illusory? – because it is changing; anything that changes is of no use, is worthless. Only the permanent, that which always remains the same, is significant. And you cannot find anything in the world that always remains the same.

Naturally, people like Adi Shankara, who has influenced India the most – all the Hindu monks that you see in India are followers of the Shankara. His whole approach is based on the emphasis that the world is an illusion because it is impermanent. "Seek the permanent and renounce the impermanent." More or less, that is the attitude of all the religions of the world.

Nietzsche, following Zarathustra, is the only contemporary who raises a great question that the idea of permanence may be just an idea because there is nothing which seems to be permanent. Except change, everything changes – unless you want change to be God, because that is the only permanent thing in the world. You cannot find anything else which can even give a hint of a permanent God.

Zarathustra is very strange. His insight is very clean and clear. He says, "who love life" because life is a changing thing. It is every moment a flux. When you came into this Chuang Tzu Hall you were another person; when you leave this Chuang Tzu Hall you will not be the same person. You only appear to be the same.

In these two hours, so much changes in you. It is just like in two hours the Ganges has been taking so much water, miles down... Although it still appears the same, it is not the same water that was there two hours before.

Heraclitus would have agreed with Zarathustra, but he was not aware of Zarathustra's existence. He is the only Western philosopher who says that life is a flux, a river. And remember, you cannot step in the same river twice because it will not be the same.

And to me too, who love life, it seems that butterflies and soap bubbles, and whatever is like them among men, know most about happiness. The people who know most about happiness are those who are in rapport with the changing life, who can even love soap bubbles, shining in the sun, creating small rainbows. These are the people who know most about happiness.

Your saints know only misery – just look at their faces. It seems life has disappeared from them, they are dead fossils. Nothing changes in them; they live a life of ritual and they are condemners of everything that changes.

Why is pleasure condemned? – because it is changing. Why is love condemned? – because it is changing. Why have these religions created marriage in place of love? It is because marriage can be given at least an illusory permanency through laws, through conventions, through society, through fear of losing respect, through fear of what will happen to our children. So they have managed to make marriage something permanent. That's why all the old religions are against divorce because divorce again exposes marriage as something impermanent – it can be changed.

For thousands of years, small children were married. There are even cases on record where children were married who were not even born, who were in their mother's womb. Two families will settle, that if a child is a boy and another child is a girl, then the marriage is settled.

In India even now, seven-year-old, eight-year-old children are married, although it is against the law. But it is not against convention. Why so much hurry to marry children who are not even aware what marriage means, what is happening. The reason is that before they become young and love arises in their hearts, marriage should have happened. So when love arises in their hearts they already have a wife – the wife already has a husband. It is to destroy love that child marriage was propagated all over the world.

It is not a coincidence that marriage creates more misery in the world than anything else because it destroys the only possibility of happiness, the happening of love. The heart never dances; people live and die without knowing love. Birth is not in your hands; death is not in your hands. Only love was your freedom: that too society has destroyed.

These are the only three things that can be major incidents of your life: birth, love and death.

Birth, you cannot control – your own birth; nobody asks you, you just find yourself born one day. And the same happens with death – it does not ask you either, "Are you ready? I am coming tomorrow." No advance notice; just suddenly it comes, and you are dead.

Only love is the freedom standing between these two. That too, society has tried to snatch away from you, so that your whole life becomes just a mechanical routine.

To see these light, foolish, dainty, affecting little souls flutter about
– that moves Zarathustra to tears and to song.

He is saying that seeing soap bubbles, seeing butterflies, seeing rosebuds dancing in the wind – seeing such light, nonserious, you could even call them ...*foolish, dainty, affecting little souls flutter about* – that is what moves Zarathustra to tears and to song. His tears are of joy, that life is so alive that it cannot be permanent – only dead things can be permanent. The more lively a thing is, the more changing it is. This changing life all around brings tears of joy to Zarathustra, and brings songs to be sung.

And he makes his central statement:

I should believe only in a God who understood how to dance.

He doesn't need any other argument; he doesn't need any other evidence, any other proof. All he wants is to know: Can your god dance? Can your god love? Can your god sing? Can your god run after butterflies? Can your god gather wildflowers and enjoy, with tears and songs? Then he is ready to accept such a god because such a god will be truly representative of life, such a god will be nothing but life itself.

The coming statements are even more difficult to digest. It needs good digestion!

Zarathustra is for strong souls. He is not for the weak and the impotent. He does not make it a quality to be meek, to be humble. Those are not qualities in his tremendously significant vision: but to be strong, to be proud of your being, to have dignity, freedom, the qualities of the lion, the qualities of the child; but never to have the qualities of a beast of burden. He is not for the patience of the camel. He is absolutely against those who are readily available to be enslaved.

> We do not wish to be spared by our best enemies, nor by those whom we love from the very heart. So let me tell you the truth!
> My brothers in war! I love you from the very heart, I am and have always been of your kind. And I am also your best enemy. So let me tell you the truth!...
> You should be such men as are always looking for an enemy – for your enemy.

This has been my experience, that when you choose a friend you need not be very cautious – anybody will do. But when you choose your enemy, you have to be very cautious. The enemy has to be someone with the best qualities possible because you are going to fight with him. And whenever you fight with someone, slowly, slowly you become exactly like your enemy.

Never choose the wrong enemy; otherwise, even in your victory, you will be defeated because you will have to learn the same strategies, the same cunningness, as your enemy. Otherwise, you cannot fight with him.

Choose the enemy who is wise, and to fight with him you have to be wise. Choose your enemy who is intelligent because to fight with him you have to be intelligent. Choose your enemy remembering perfectly that fighting with him you will become like him. Whether you are defeated or you are victorious is secondary. The primary concern should be the choice of the right enemy.

Without the enemy you don't have a challenge. This will look very strange because all the religions, and all the so-called philosophers have been teaching you, "Don't have any enemies." But that will take away all challenge to growth, all challenge to be stronger, to be great in war, to be clever, to be alert of the opportunities.

Zarathustra is not against war; that's where he differs from Gautam Buddha and Mahavira. It is for you to remember that it was only after Mahavira and Gautam Buddha, two great teachers, the highest-quality teachers, that India started falling down. It should have been otherwise. After Buddha and Mahavira, India should have risen higher – that would have been logical. It seems to be very illogical that India's fall begins with Gautam Buddha and Mahavira.

Indians have become so cowardly that they cannot even think retrospectively of what caused India's fall. In the times of Gautam Buddha, India was known all over the world as a Golden Bird. It was so rich, so intelligent, so civilized, so cultured and the West was still in the state of barbarity.

What happened? Suddenly, India started falling down. If you listen to Zarathustra, you can see the reason. Both Gautam Buddha and Mahavira taught India nonviolence: no war, but peace. Peace is a very delicate phenomenon. People were very ready for it, not because they have understood Gautam Buddha or Mahavira, but because it was a good consolation to their cowardliness. *Peacefulness* is a beautiful word to cover up your impotence.

No war seems to be a good defense, and the ultimate result was that small tribes of barbarous people, who were thousands of years behind India, conquered India – butchered people, raped the women, burned cities. India remained with the consolation: we are peaceful people, we are nonviolent people, we cannot fight.

For two thousand years, India remained a slave, not of one country, but of many countries. Whoever wanted to conquer was welcome. Such a vast country remaining a slave for two thousand years is unprecedented in the whole history of the world. There was no resistance; people behaved the way Zarathustra describes the camels. They sat down, and they asked to be loaded, and they felt it a great happiness that they were carrying the heaviest load. The camel who was carrying the heaviest load became the hero. And India became poor; it lost its guts.

Zarathustra has to be understood very deeply: he's not saying that you have to be violent, he's not saying that you have to kill, and he's not saying that you have to destroy. That would be a misunderstanding. That misunderstanding happened to Adolf Hitler. These were the sentences which created the Second World War, but Adolf Hitler could not understand the delicate and the subtle meaning of Zarathustra.

Zarathustra is saying that you need not be aggressive, you need not be destructive, but you have to always be prepared. If you want peace, your bow and arrow should be ready.

He's not saying that you start killing. He's saying that if worst comes to worst, the enemy should not be left to destroy you, to rape your women, to destroy your property, to take away your dignity, to make you slaves.

My brothers in war! I love you from the very heart, I am, and have always been, of your kind. If one really wants to be nonviolent, one should be a warrior, one should be a samurai, one should know the art of swordsmanship, and one should know archery – not to kill anyone, but just to protect one's dignity, one's freedom; it is such a simple logic.

But India has not understood even now. Nobody blames our ideology of nonviolence for making us weak, defenseless, vulnerable. It has taken away our very force and strength to resist against anyone who wants to enslave us.

And I am also your best enemy. That sentence will make it clear. On the one hand, he says: *My brothers in war! I love you from the very heart, I am and always have been of your kind.* I am a warrior, and still I want to say to you: *And I am also your best enemy.* Because I am not aggressive. Remember, I am a warrior. To put it differently, one has to be a nonaggressive warrior; only then can one protect his dignity and his freedom.

So let me tell you the truth!...
You should be such men as are always looking for an enemy...

You should always be preparing as if you are looking for the enemy.

...for your enemy. And with some of you there is hate at first sight.

In the beginning, your being a warrior will have some color of hate in it, but that is your weakness. One has to be a warrior without any hate. One has to be a warrior just as a sport, with the sportsman's spirit – not to fight because of hate, but to fight for the sheer joy. The challenge should not go unreplied.

You should seek your enemy, you should wage your war – a war for
your opinions.

And it is not only the ordinary war in which you fight with arms;
you should also seek your enemy for your opinions.

I have been around the world, challenging all kinds of prejudices, challenging all kinds of opinions which according to me are
nothing but lies – ancient lies. But the world has become completely
without warriors; nobody will accept the challenge. On the contrary,
they will close the doors of their country, they will not let me in –
these are the cowards.

I have come to their country. I am alone. Their church has the
whole country behind it; and the government behind it, the army
and all the weapons with them. I am empty handed, I have just my
understanding of truth, and I want to discuss with those people who
have been dominating those countries for thousands of years. But
they are such cowards that rather than accepting my challenge, they
pressurize their governments, their parliaments to pass laws that I
cannot enter their country.

It was not so in the past, particularly in this country. Mystics used
to move around the country, challenging anybody who had opposite
opinions for a public discussion. And those discussions were not with
any hatred, they were full of reverence for each other, respect for
each other. They were not to prove: I am right and you are wrong.
Instead, they were a search, together, to know what truth is.

Truth is not mine, and cannot be yours. But it is possible that my
opinion may be closer to truth, and your opinion may not be so
close; or your opinion may be closer to truth, and my opinion may
not be so close.

These discussions around the country raised the level of consciousness and intelligence of people. People heard their great
thinkers wrestling with each other, with subtle logic. The whole
atmosphere was freedom of expression, and freedom to convince
others, or to be convinced by others. The war of opinions is truly
the real war. The war with arms is ugly, is animal; but the war
between opinions, philosophies, religions is to raise the whole of
humanity higher.

But people have become so impotent in every direction that if you
say anything that goes against somebody's prejudice, immediately

he goes to the court. He does not come to me; he goes to the court: "My religious feeling is hurt."

Almost all the time, there are at least a dozen cases going on all over the country against me. Just now in Kanpur, they have put a case against me in the court – ten Christian associations together – that I have hurt their feelings because in one of my statements I said, "The Bible is a pornographic book."

Now those people don't understand that in the court, they will look idiots. There are five hundred pages in the whole Bible, not less than that, which are pornographic. I am sending those five hundred pages to my advocate, so that there is no need to argue. He can just present those pages, and ask these people, "Are these pornographic, or not?"

If these are not pornographic, then nothing can be pornographic, and if these are pornographic, then the Holy Bible is the most unholy book in the world, and it should be banned in every country.

But it is not only about the Bible, the same is the case with Hindu *puranas* – so ugly, so obscene. Fortunately, nobody reads them.

But I am not so fortunate; these are not good times for the intellectual growth of humanity. If any statement hurts your religious feeling, first look into your religious book – I am not hurting your religious feeling: your Bible is. I am simply quoting from the Bible. The Christians should burn the Bible because it is hurting their religious feelings.

If your religious feeling is hurt, that shows only a weakness. You should have courage enough to argue. They should have written articles against me, but they cannot because they know that in the Bible there are pornographic portions. They should have challenged me for a public discussion; and I was ready for a public discussion in Kanpur – in their churches.

For me, it is not a problem at all – I just have to open their Bible at random, I can open and read. There is no need to remember which pages – the pornography is spread all over it. But even to say something, howsoever truthful it may be, immediately they go to the court. What kind of camels? They want the law to support them; they don't have any logic to support them. One goes to the court only when he has no means of supporting himself intelligently.

I have been speaking my whole life. I have never been heard. And so much is written against me – lies and condemnations without any foundation in truth. But I have not gone to any court; I can answer those people myself. Once anybody goes to the court against me, then I make it a point to hit him harder, and more often until he's completely silent.

The world needs warriors of intelligence:

...and if your opinion is defeated, your honesty should still cry triumph over that!

Don't be worried even *...if your opinion is defeated...* at least your honesty will be your triumph.

You should love peace as a means to new wars.

You should not become a pacifist because to become a pacifist is to become victim to those who do not believe in pacifism. You should love peace, but you should always be ready for new wars. Those wars need not happen, but you should not relax your bow, and you should not forget your arrows. Your swords should not collect dust. You should be ready always for war, ordinary war, or intellectual war; but your readiness should be there. Your very readiness will give you a beauty, and a grace.

And the short peace more than the long.

The longer the peace, the more one relaxes, the more one starts thinking that there is going to be no war. One should be aware that war can be any moment, on any level.

I do not exhort you to work but to battle. I do not exhort you to peace, but to victory. May your work be a battle, may your peace be a victory!
One can be silent and sit still only when one has arrow and bow; otherwise, one babbles and quarrels. May your peace be a victory!
You say it is the good cause that hallows even war?

Zarathustra is certainly a man of tremendously great insights.

You say it is the good cause that hallows even war? I tell you: it is the good war that hallows every cause.

It is not the good cause of communism, democracy, Christianity, Islam, Hinduism, God – these are "good causes" for which people have been warring for thousands of years.

But Zarathustra says that it is not the good causes that make the wars holy, that make the wars crusades; on the contrary, it is the good war, a war which is an art in itself, that hallows every cause.

In fact, I am against nuclear weapons, atomic weapons, bombs because these are ugly things; they don't make men warriors. A nuclear missile can destroy the whole country – there is no question of any fight. We should drown all those weapons in the Atlantic. We should move back to swords, and teach people swordsmanship. We should move back to the bow and arrow because that gives dignity to man, an athletic beauty to man; and it is not destructive.

It has been found, particularly in Japan where they have developed swordsmanship with meditation, and archery also with meditation, that if two swordsmen who are both deeply meditative are fighting, they can go on fighting for hours – nobody will be killed. They both have the same intuitive sense. Before the other attacks, your sword will be ready to protect you.

It has happened many times in the history of Japan that equal meditators fighting with swords have not been able to defeat anyone. But both have been victorious because both have shown the art, and their intuition. And the same is with archery.

Those are human means because they dignify you. Bombs – nuclear, atomic and others – can be dropped even by a plane without a pilot; the plane can be controlled remotely. The plane will come to the target, drop the bombs, and return to its airport. But this is sheer destructiveness, stupid destructiveness. It is not war, it is pure violence; it is a suicide which should be avoided.

Wars should not be condemned; the weapons that we have developed should be condemned. War as such is an art, like any other art: painting, music, dance, architecture; so is archery, swordsmanship, wrestling.

If peace reigns over the world – no battle, no war, no challenge – human beings will become pygmies; then there is no possibility of metamorphosis. Then camels will become even uglier, and will forget completely that they have a possibility to become lions.

War and courage have done more great things than charity.

In fact, just like Zarathustra, I hate charity because the basic idea of charity is ugly; it humiliates human beings. But Christianity has made it so prominent that even other religions, who had never thought about it, are following. They have to because charity has become almost equivalent to religiousness.

But charity has not created anything great in the world, that is true. How many orphans of Mother Theresa have proved to be geniuses? How many orphans have become musicians? How many orphans have proved to be scientists? How many orphans have proved their dignity in any dimension of life?

In fact, from the very beginning their dignity has been taken away, they are orphans; their souls have been killed. Rather than having charity, it is better not to have orphans. And orphans can be prevented; there is no need for orphans. Poverty can be prevented; there is no need to throw alms to the poor.

First, you make the poor, and then you give charity to the poor; it is such a great deception. All the richest people of the world have their own trusts and foundations for charity. On the other hand, they go on exploiting people. Otherwise, from where does their super-richness come?

For example, perhaps you may have never thought about this: the Nobel Prize is being given to people who create peace, who serve the poor, who create great literature, or scientific inventions – and with each Prize goes almost a quarter of a million dollars. But do you know from where this money has come? The man in whose name the Nobel Prize is being given, earned his whole money in the First World War by creating weapons. He was the greatest manufacturer of weapons in the world.

By his weapons, millions of people were killed. And with all the money that he accumulated, he created a foundation, a charity, and now every year all the Nobel Prizes are given, just from the interest on the money. The original money remains in the bank, just the interest – and nobody bothers that this money is blood soaked. And the name of Nobel has become one of the greatest names in history.

Charity is a strange game: first you cripple people and then you help them. First you destroy their environment, their ecology, and then from the same people who have been destroying the ecology of the earth, comes the money for charity.

The pope goes on teaching against birth control. And it is only the poor people who create more children; rich people don't create more children because they have other enjoyments in life. The poor man has nowhere else to go when he comes back home because everywhere – if he goes to a disco, or a restaurant, or a movie – money is needed. Sex is his only free entertainment.

He creates dozens of children. The pope goes on telling people that to prevent children is an act against God. And then poverty goes on growing; then charity is needed, then these poor people cannot afford... They leave their children by the side of the road. All the orphans that Mother Theresa goes on collecting are from the streets of Kolkata. People simply leave their children on the street – even a one-day-old baby.

Mother Theresa's seven hundred sisters, sisters of charity, go on collecting these babies. Mother Theresa goes on around the world collecting funds to raise these orphans. And then these orphans will produce more children – strange games.

Poverty can be prevented. Anything that needs charity should be prevented – charity is an ugly concept. Sharing is another thing. You share with your equals. Charity means degrading the other person.

Zarathustra is right:

War and courage have done more great things than charity. Not your pity but your bravery has saved the unfortunate up to now.... Thus live your life of obedience and war! What good is long life? What warrior wants to be spared?

Long life is not the goal. Even if you have a small life, have it in its totality, have it in its intensity – make it a song, make it a dance. Just the length of life is absolutely meaningless. The depth of life has intrinsic value.

These are statements which will go against your prejudices. First you will have to understand them before your prejudices start distorting them, disturbing them, changing their color, interpreting them. Keep your prejudices away; first, try to understand what he means. And once you have understood, you will not think that he is for war. He is not for violence, he is not for destruction.

But he does not want man to lose the qualities of the warrior. He does not want man to become a coward. He does not want man incapable of accepting challenges in life, whether they are of war or of intellectual opinions.

Man should be ready always: his sword should be sharp, and his intelligence should be sharp too; only then can there be peace. When everybody is so intelligent, so artful, and so ready to die – though not to be enslaved – only then will the world know a peace that will not be the peace of the graveyard. It will be the peace of a beautiful garden, where birds sing, and flowers blossom, and a cool breeze comes.

Life, not death, should be your goal. And a life that is enriched by love, a life that is ready for any emergency, a life one can live dangerously without any fear.

First try to understand Zarathustra, and let his meaning go deeper into your being. Then you can allow your prejudices to come in, and you will find your prejudices are empty.

Zarathustra may be alone, but truth is with him: you may be with the whole world, but truth is not with you.

...Thus spake Zarathustra.

CHAPTER 5

infinite capacity to enjoy

Of the Compassionate

As long as men have existed, man has enjoyed himself too little: that alone, my brothers, is our original sin!

And if we learn better to enjoy ourselves, we best unlearn how to do harm to others and to contrive harm.

Therefore I wash my hand when it has helped a sufferer, therefore I wipe my soul clean as well.

For I saw the sufferer suffer, and because I saw it I was ashamed on account of his shame; and when I helped him, then I sorely injured his pride....

"Be reserved in accepting! Honor a man by accepting from him!" – thus I advise those who have nothing to give.

I, however, am a giver: I give gladly as a friend to friends. But strangers and the poor may pluck the fruit from my tree for themselves: it causes less shame that way....

And we are the most unfair, not towards him whom we do not like, but towards him for whom we feel nothing at all.

But if you have a suffering friend, be a resting-place for his suffering, but a resting-place like a hard bed, a camp-bed: thus you will serve him best.

*And should your friend do you a wrong, then say: "I forgive you
what you did to me; but that you did it to yourself – how could I
forgive that?"
Thus speaks all great love: it overcomes even forgiveness and pity....
Alas, where in the world have there been greater follies than with
the compassionate? And what in the world has caused more
suffering than the follies of the compassionate?
Woe to all lovers who cannot surmount pity!
Thus spoke the devil to me once: "Even God has his Hell: it is his
love for man...."
So be warned against pity: thence shall yet come a heavy cloud for
man! Truly, I understand weather-signs!
But mark, too, this saying: All great love is above pity: for it wants
– to create what is loved!
"I offer myself to my love,* and my neighbor as myself" – *that is
the language of all creators.
All creators, however, are hard.*

...Thus spake Zarathustra.

The original sin has been discussed by almost all religions. They all have different ideas about it. The most prominent and prevalent is the Christian idea. According to Christianity, disobedience is the original sin. The moment one decides that disobedience is the original sin, obedience automatically becomes the greatest virtue. Obedience creates slaves. Obedience is a poison that destroys all possibility of rebellion. Obedience is destructive, destructive of the very dignity of man.

The Christian story is beautiful, although an absolute lie. God, in the very beginning, had forbidden man to eat from the trees of wisdom and of eternal life. The very idea seems to be absurd. On the one hand God is the creator, the father, and on the other hand he is prohibiting his own children from being wise and living eternally. There seems to be a great contradiction.

The Devil persuades Eve to eat from the tree of wisdom, and his argument is absolutely rational, human, and tremendously significant. He says to Eve that if you don't eat from the tree of wisdom and from the tree of eternal life, you will always remain animals; and God is afraid that if you eat from the tree of wisdom and the tree of eternal life, you will become gods. He is jealous, jealous of his own children. He is afraid. He does not want you to transcend your animal existence, he wants you to remain ignorant, unconscious, dependent, while you have the potential of being equals of God.

His argument is so profound that it seems the Christian God is not behaving the way a god is supposed to behave. On the contrary, the Devil is behaving in a more divine way. In fact, the word *devil* comes from a Sanskrit root which means divine. The word *divine* comes from the same root.

But Eve and Adam rebelled. And as God became aware that they had eaten the fruit of wisdom, he immediately expelled them from the Garden of Eden, afraid that now they will eat from the other tree which will make them eternal beings, immortal.

The story is significant in many ways because the whole history of man is nothing but an inquiry into gaining more and more wisdom, and an inquiry into finding the eternal sources of life.

All the religions have been trying to make it that man should not go against the commandments that are coming from God, although the commandments are ugly. Man is expected to say yes in spite of himself; only his obedience and faith are going to deliver him. This has made the whole of humanity remain retarded, unevolved. Having all the treasures and yet living in misery, having all the potential to reach to the stars, but still crawling on the earth.

All the religions without exception have deprived man of his pride. And the moment man loses his pride, his dignity, he loses his very soul; he falls below the human level of life to sub-human levels.

Zarathustra brings a new light as far as the original sin is concerned, and he seems to be the most relevant and rational amongst all the other mystics of the world. What he says is so pure, so clear, so undeniably true that it needs no argument to prove it; it is self-evident, it is self-luminous.

Says he:

As long as men have existed, man has enjoyed himself too little: that alone, my brothers, is our original sin!

You have such an infinite capacity to enjoy the whole rainbow of pleasures, happinesses, joys, and blessings. But all the religions have been telling you to renounce pleasures, renounce life, live as minimally as possible. Don't live, just survive. And this has become the way of their saints. This they call austerity, this they call discipline: to wash away the original sin that Adam and Eve committed.

Zarathustra is exceptional, and can be understood only by very intelligent and very exceptional people. That's why, as far as numbers are concerned, there is not a great religion following Zarathustra. There are millions of people who have not even heard his name, and he has given greater original insights than anybody else.

Do you recognize the originality? He is saying the only original sin is that man has allowed himself to enjoy too little! He has not lived totally, intensely, madly. He has not lived with his whole being, he has not been orgasmic. And even if he has enjoyed a little bit, he has enjoyed it full of fear – he will be punished for it. Torturing yourself is going to be rewarded in the other world; enjoying yourself will lead you into an abysmal hell where you will be tortured eternally; forever and forever.

So even though man has enjoyed a little, there was fear; it was always half-hearted, he was never total in it, he never got lost in it. The religions have not been able to take man away from pleasures completely, but they have succeeded almost ninety-nine percent. And whatsoever has remained – that one percent – they have poisoned it. You enjoyed, knowing perfectly well you were committing a sin and you were paving a path toward hell.

And why does Zarathustra call it the original sin? – because a man who has not enjoyed at the maximum, at the optimum, will not know what life is all about, will not know what is virtue, will not know the significance and the beauty of existence. He will remain ignorant, he will remain psychologically sick because your whole nature is demanding pleasure and your mind, contaminated by the priests, is holding you back.

Every man is in a strange tension. Nature wants to go in one direction and your religions want to take you in the exact opposite direction. Your whole life becomes a fight with yourself. You become your own enemy. And unless you know life in its heights – pleasures transforming into blissfulness, enjoyment turning into ecstasies – you are committing an original sin against life itself.

And if we learn better to enjoy ourselves, we best unlearn how to do harm to others and to contrive harm.

Zarathustra comes to strange conclusions, from very novel directions. Gautam Buddha says, "Do not harm anybody. Do not hurt anybody because that is a sin." Mahavira says, "Violence of any kind is a sin." Zarathustra comes to the same conclusion, but his whole argument is more profound than Gautam Buddha and Mahavira. *And if we learn better to enjoy ourselves, we best unlearn how to do harm to others and to contrive harm.*

I can say with absolute authority that once you are blissful, you cannot harm anybody. Once you have known the eternity of life, and the joyous dance of life, it is impossible for you to harm anyone because there is no one other than you. We are not separate islands; we are one continent, one single whole.

He is not making it a sin, he is not prohibiting you from harming others. He is simply saying, enjoy yourself to the fullest and you will not harm others because in your very enjoyment the idea of *I* and *thou* disappears. There are no longer others; it is one life in millions of manifestations. In the trees, in the animals, in human beings, in the stars – these are all manifestations of one life, one single life.

If we are harming anybody, we are harming ourselves. But this insight arises in you when you reach to the highest peak of bliss. That's why he says, "Man's original sin is that he has enjoyed himself too little." And a man who has not enjoyed himself will not tolerate anybody else enjoying himself.

These are simple psychological facts. The man who is in pain, in anguish, in anxiety, in misery, cannot tolerate anybody else being blissful. It hurts. Why am I miserable and why are others not? And if the whole of humanity is suffering, then to be blissful in this suffering humanity is to be constantly in danger.

People would like to destroy you. You don't belong to them, you are not miserable enough. You are a stranger. Perhaps you are mad because when the whole world is so miserable how can you manage to laugh? How can you manage to dance and sing?

Just the other day Neelam brought many articles: a few for me, a few against me, a few neutral. Every day she brings them. It is amazing; I don't even read them. All over the world, in all the languages, people are taking so much trouble – writing for me, writing against me, writing neutrally, being factual. In one article she simple read one line in it. Because I have been seeing them, she feels embarrassed and hurt because people are writing absolute lies about me, not even a fragment of truth in them. So she simply says, "This is disgusting, nasty," and throws it away. And before throwing away that article, she said, "This man is writing utter lies."

One thing, in the beginning he says I am the most-disrespected and the most-learned man of the day. He will be shocked, whoever has written it, because I don't want to be respected by sheep and goats, by monkeys and donkeys, by pigs and pygmies. I have never in my life desired any respect. I don't consider the present humanity worthy enough to have its respect, it is enough to have its disrespect. The men whom Zarathustra calls supermen – perhaps they will be able to respect me because they will be able to understand me. Even today there are a few people who understand me; and then their respect is not only respect, it is love, it is devotion.

And as far as being the most learned, that man is absolutely wrong. I do not belong to the category of the learned. My whole life has been based on a fundamental truth which can only be called unlearning. Whatever the society has forced me to learn, through the schools and the colleges and the universities, my work has been how to unlearn it; how to clean myself from all this junk, rubbish and all kinds of crap. I am not a learned man. Perhaps I might be the most-unlearned man in the world. And I would hate to be respected by the present humanity – it does not have that intelligence, nor has it that heart, nor has it that being.

Twenty-five centuries have passed and Zarathustra is not yet understood, is not even now loved and respected. Perhaps the man who can love people like Zarathustra has yet to come. The clarity, the intelligence, the silence which is needed to understand him is absolutely missing in present-day human beings.

The reason it is missing is that they have not allowed themselves to actualize all their potential. They have not allowed themselves to go the way of nature, the way of the Tao; they have not allowed themselves to flow with the stream. They have listened to wrong people, who have been teaching them to swim upstream, in which they are going to be frustrated and they are going to be failures – and then they become condemners. The moment a person fails in achieving his goal he becomes a condemner. And because everybody has been told to make goals, which are anti-life, anti-pleasure, anti-nature – failure is absolutely certain.

These miserable people cannot understand a blissful man, and the man who has not known bliss enjoys only one thing, the suffering of others. Every morning he is waiting for the newspaper just to know how many crimes have been committed, how many people have been murdered, how many people have committed suicide. Because good news is no news, only something bad, something disgusting is news. Anything natural is not news, howsoever beautiful it may be.

Just the opposite happens when you are blissful: you want everybody else to be blissful too because your blissfulness becomes multiplied by everybody else being blissful too. Harming anybody becomes simply impossible. It is not a discipline, it is not a vow that you have taken in a temple according to any religion; it is a simple outcome of your own blissfulness that you cannot harm. You know life enjoys itself in being blissful, how can you destroy any other life? Just as you enjoy, every form of life wants to enjoy.

Certainly, if everything around you is dancing and ecstatic, it is going to make your own ecstasy far richer. The reward is here, now. Harming others becomes impossible because it is harming your own joy. And helping people to be blissful is not to be a service to them, but a service to yourself because their joy is going to enhance your joy. The more people are blissful in the world, the more there is an atmosphere of celebration. In that atmosphere you can dance more easily, you can sing more easily. This is a great contribution of Zarathustra.

> *Therefore I wash my hand when it has helped a sufferer, therefore I wipe my soul clean as well.*
> *For I saw the sufferer suffer, and because I saw it I was ashamed on account of his shame; and when I helped him, then I sorely injured his pride.*

He is always original in seeing things. The same things have been seen by millions of people, but Zarathustra finds an angle which is absolutely virgin. He is saying, "Whenever I help somebody who is suffering, I know I am hurting his pride, I know he is feeling shame that he is suffering. Because of his shame I feel ashamed, and because I have helped him I have sorely injured his pride."

Rather than expecting to have pleasures in heaven because he has helped somebody who is suffering – opening an account in paradise, counting on one's virtues – he says, "I wash my hand because I have hurt somebody's pride. I have seen him suffer, I have seen him naked, I have seen his wounds, which he was hiding. Although I have helped him – but what is my help? His pride is hurt, and I have to wash my hands. I have to do something so that he does not feel ashamed, so he does not feel that his pride has been hurt; on the contrary, he feels that he has obliged me, he has given me an opportunity to help a brother. He is not obliged to me, I am obliged to him."

"Be reserved in accepting! Honor a man by accepting from him!"

Be reserved, be very, very careful and cautious in accepting. *"Honor a man by accepting from him!"* It may be a small thing, a roseflower, or just a good morning, or a handshake, but accept it with such love, with such grace. He has honored you. Let him feel that he has been accepted.

In this world millions of people are suffering because nobody accepts them. Everybody asks them, "Are you worthy? Do you deserve?" Nobody accepts them as they are, and certainly, everybody is whatever he is. It is not his fault existence needs him the way he is; he must be fulfilling a certain need of which you are not aware. You are not aware of many mysteries of life, and if life is accepting a man, who are you to reject him?

But all around the world people are suffering for a simple reason that they don't have anything to give, that nobody wants them as they are, that everybody demands them to be somebody else – then they will be accepted. And nobody can be somebody else. In the very effort he becomes crippled, in the very effort he becomes distorted, in the very effort he loses his natural grace and his natural destiny, he goes astray. And this creates misery.

> *...thus I advise those who have nothing to give.*
> *I, however, am a giver: I give gladly as a friend to friends. But strangers and the poor may pluck the fruit from my tree for themselves: it causes less shame that way.*

Do you see his insight? He says, "I give to my friends because it will not hurt their pride. They will rejoice with me. I have accepted things from them; I have accepted them, they will accept me. But to the poor, but to strangers, I would suggest it is better they: ...*pluck the fruit from my tree for themselves: it causes less shame that way.*

Their pride will not be hurt, and they will not feel inferior to me. It is very difficult to find a man of deeper insight into human psychology.

And we are the most unfair, not towards him whom we do not like, but towards him for whom we feel nothing at all.

You can love someone, you can hate someone, but don't be neutral, don't be indifferent. You can like, you can dislike – in either case you are taking a standpoint. But don't say, "It does not matter to me." The moment you become neutral you are simply saying that whether that man exists or dies it makes no difference to you.

This is the greatest harm that you can do to somebody. Hate will not hurt so much. At least you hate, there is a relationship. And hate can turn into love at any moment because love turns into hate – they are convertible. Likings can become dislikings tomorrow and vice versa, but indifference remains indifference.

Indifference is the worst kind of behavior a man can adopt. But watch yourself, how indifferent are you? How many people do you love, how many people do you hate? How many people do you like, how many people do you dislike? The number will be very small. And what about the millions to whom you are simply indifferent? In Ethiopia if one thousand people die every day, you simply read it in the newspaper and you don't lose even a heartbeat. Ethiopia is far away, it is almost another planet; and obviously you cannot care about the whole world.

It is not a question of care. It is a question of the expansion of your consciousness. Ethiopia should be part of the map of your consciousness. But in Ethiopia people were dying because they had no food, and in Europe food was being destroyed in the ocean because they had superfluous food – mountains of butter, mountains of food-stuff. Just the cost of destruction was two billion dollars. That was not the cost of the food – it was just the cost of taking the food to the ocean and throwing it into the ocean. One wonders, does man really have a heart, or is it just a fiction?

The same was happening in America. Every six months in Europe and America – both places – billions of dollars are wasted in destroying food, and in the poor countries people are dying. And death by starvation is the ugliest because it takes such a long time, and so much unnecessary suffering. A healthy man can live without food for three months, then he will die. But those three months will be hell, they will appear like three lives.

A man who knows life as a joy will also understand that other living beings are in the same category; they also want to live, they also want to enjoy. If I can do something it is not for them, it is not a service – it is just my joy, my pleasure to share myself.

> But if you have a suffering friend, be a resting-place for his suffering, but a resting-place like a hard bed, a camp-bed: thus you will serve him best.
> And should your friend do you a wrong, then say: "I forgive you what you did to me; but that you did it to yourself – how could I forgive that?"

What can I do about that? Doing something to me you have done something to yourself, too. I can forgive you for what you have done to me, but what can I do about what you have done to yourself? You cannot hurt anybody without hurting yourself. It is just impossible to behave in a disgusting way with anybody; you are at the same time behaving disgustingly with yourself.

You cannot insult somebody without insulting yourself.

> Thus speaks all great love: it overcomes even forgiveness and pity.

When you say, "I pity," it is not love because to whomsoever you show your pity, you make him feel inferior. Love never makes anybody feel inferior. It gives superiority. It brings out the best in the other. Pity and service to the poor are ugly words; duty...these are not words of love. These are the conveniences of a miserable society. These are not the sharings of a blissful world.

> Alas, where in the world have there been greater follies than with the compassionate? And what in the world has caused more suffering than the follies of the compassionate?

You may have never thought that compassion can also cause

misery. But that's what it has done. Mohammedans have killed millions of people out of compassion. Christians have killed millions of people out of compassion. The compassion for the Mohammedan is that if you are not a Mohammedan, then become a Mohammedan because only a Mohammedan will be saved on the last day of judgment. Even if you have to be forced on the point of a sword, it is compassion. And if you are still unwilling to become a Mohammedan, it is better that you are killed because to be killed at the hands of a Mohammedan you have some chance of being saved.

Christian missionaries go on spreading in the world that unless you are a Christian you cannot be saved. There is only one savior, Jesus Christ. Those who don't follow Jesus have to be brought somehow into the fold. In the past, they used to be forced by violence, by murder, by arson. Today the means of converting them has changed, but the basic idea remains the same. First, they used to come with a Bible in one hand and a sword in the other; now they come with a Bible in one hand and a loaf of bread in the other.

The hungry, the starving cannot resist the temptation. Even if he has to become a Christian – he does not know anything about religion, his whole life he has known only one thing and that is hunger. The bread certainly seems to be a great redemption. But by giving bread to the poor you are purchasing their souls. And the idea is, the more people you make Christian, the more you accumulate virtue. You are not concerned with their being saved, you are concerned with your own account, your own virtue. Compassion has done much harm. The coming man has to rise above compassion. The new man has to learn sharing – not for any reward, not for any compensation, but just out of sheer joy. It is joy to share. If you have bread and you can share with a hungry man without hurting his pride, if you can share with those who are unfortunate and yet remain graceful, that will be true virtue.

Woe to all lovers who cannot surmount pity!
Thus spoke the devil to me once: "Even God has his Hell: it is his love for man."

It is a very strange statement. Zarathustra is speaking through the mouth of the Devil because he cannot say it directly. He cannot say it directly because he has declared God to be dead. And if God is dead the Devil cannot survive, they both are fictions, complementary to each other; they can only exist together. But just to make a significant statement he uses the metaphor of the Devil: *Thus spoke the devil to me once: "Even God has his Hell: it is his love for man."*

It reminds me of Jean-Paul Sartre, who was one of the most significant philosophers of our century. He says, "The other is hell." And it is the conclusion of a long life of many love affairs; but each love affair ended in a state of hell. Finally he draws the conclusion that it does not matter who the other is, the other itself is hell. The other has his own likings, dislikings; even lovers cannot be in harmony because harmony is a totally different discipline. Unless you have learned to be in harmony with yourself, how you can be in harmony with anybody else?

So it is good if lovers just meet on the beaches, in the parks – just once in a while. Everything seems to be great and beautiful because both are alert and keeping on their masks, their makeup; they are saying sweet nothings to each other.

But once they start living together it becomes difficult to go on being false twenty-four hours a day. It becomes heavy, and the mask goes on slipping; you cannot hold it on for twenty-four hours. And you cannot go on saying the same old sweet nothings again and again – they become boring. Soon you find there is nothing to talk about. Your love becomes a repetition, a mechanical repetition, as if you are seeing the same old film again and again and again.

I have heard about a villager...

When a movie, a touring movie, came for the first time to his village, he saw the matinee show. Everybody had left, but he was sitting there. The manager came, "What is the idea? The show is finished, and now we will have to clean for the next show."

The villager said, "You can bring the ticket for the next show, I am not going anywhere, I will see the next show. And if I am not satisfied, I will see the third show also." There were three shows every day.

The manager thought the man seemed mad, but he gave money, so he said, "Perhaps, let him see it." After the second show, the manager came again just out of curiosity to ask, "Are you satisfied?"

The villager said, "Satisfied? My foot! I have to see the third show also. Here is the money, bring the ticket."

But the manager said, "What is the problem? If I can be of any help..."

He said, "Nobody can be of any help. But I'm not going to go unless I'm satisfied."

The manager said, "What is your satisfaction? How can you be satisfied? Just tell me."

The villager said, "In the film, there is a beautiful woman just standing on the bank of a beautiful lake, undressing. She's almost undressed, just the last piece of cloth has remained; and unfortunately, a train comes and by the time the train has passed, the woman is swimming in the lake. I'm waiting because, in India, it is impossible for the train to come always at the right time. Someday it is going to be late; if not today, tomorrow, I will come. The day after tomorrow I will come. One day it is going to happen that the train will not come, only then I will be satisfied."

The manager said, "My God, it is going to be very difficult!"

But what are you seeing in your film? – the same film, and even the train does not come. And every night you decide enough is enough, but after twenty-four hours you start thinking perhaps, one never knows, something may be different. And it has been going on for your whole life.

The moment anything becomes a repetition you start behaving like a robot. And everything is bound to become a repetition, unless your intelligence, your meditativeness, your love is so great that it goes on transforming yourself and the person you love; so that each time you look in the eyes of the person you love, it is something different, it is something new – new flowers have blossomed, the season has changed.

Unless one remains changing, even love becomes hell. Otherwise, everybody in the whole world would be in love, but everybody is living in his own hell – private hells, just like attached bathrooms. To live a life which never becomes a misery, which never becomes a hell, one has to be fresh every moment, unburdened of the past, always trying to find new dimensions to relate with people, new ways to relate with people, new songs to sing. One should make it a point, a basic point, that you will not live like a machine because the machine has no life – it has efficiency. The world needs you to be a machine because the world needs efficiency.

But your own being needs you to be absolutely non-mechanical, unpredictable – each morning should find you new. That is the way of the superman. That is the way of the sannyasin.

> *So be warned against pity: thence shall yet come a heavy cloud for man! Truly, I understand weather-signs!*
> *But mark, too, this saying: All great love is above pity: for it wants – to create what is loved!*

Pity, sympathy, compassion are far lower than love because love is a creative experience. Lovers create each other. In their creating each other continuously, they remain new, they remain fresh.

> *"I offer myself to my love, and* my neighbor as myself...."

Never deceive your love because no deception is going to be unknown, undiscovered; soon the other will come to know your deception. Never lie to the person you love; be authentic and be sincere, and be just an open book – not hiding anything, not pretending anything. Remain yourself.

"I offer myself to my love, and my neighbor as myself...." Hence, there is no need of feeling a burden of pretensions, lies, deceptions, hypocrisies. Just be authentically yourself.

> *...that is the language of all creators.*
> *All creators, however, are hard.*

Love as creativity is a tremendously significant idea. Love not only as a relationship between two static persons, but love as a creative whirlpool, love as a dance, so fast, at full speed, that it is difficult to find who is the lover and who is the beloved. And the dance goes on becoming deeper and deeper, and the dancers disappear and only the dance remains. One can make his life a beautiful dance, a creative act of love.

Zarathustra teaches love as the highest value. Love to him is God, love to him is religion.

> *...Thus spake Zarathustra.*

knowledge is cheap, knowing is costly

Of Scholars

...I have left the house of scholars and slammed the door behind me.

Too long did my soul sit hungry at their table; I have not been schooled, as they have, to crack knowledge as one cracks nuts.

I love freedom and the air over fresh soil; I would sleep on ox-skins rather than on their dignities and respectabilities.

I am too hot and scorched by my own thought: it is often about to take my breath away. Then I have to get into the open air and away from all dusty rooms.

But they sit cool in the cool shade: they want to be mere spectators in everything and they take care not to sit where the sun burns upon the steps....

When they give themselves out as wise, their little sayings and truths make me shiver: their wisdom often smells as if it came from the swamp....

They are clever, they have cunning fingers: what is my simplicity compared with their diversity? Their fingers understand all threading and knitting and weaving: thus they weave the stockings of the spirit!...

*They keep a sharp eye upon one another and do not trust one
another as well as they might. Inventive in small slynesses, they lie
in wait for those whose wills go upon lame feet – they lie in wait
like spiders....*
*They also know how to play with loaded dice; and I found them
playing so zealously that they were sweating.*
*We are strangers to one another, and their virtues are even more
opposed to my taste than are their falsehoods and loaded dice.*
*And when I lived among them I lived above them. They grew angry
with me for that.*
*They did not want to know that someone was walking over their
heads; and so they put wood and dirt and rubbish between their
heads and me.*
*Thus they muffled the sound of my steps: and from then on the
most scholarly heard me the worst....*
*But I walk above their heads with my thoughts in spite of that; and
even if I should walk upon my own faults, I should still be above
them and their heads.*
*For men are not equal: thus speaks justice. And what I desire they
may not desire!*

...Thus spake Zarathustra.

One of the most important distinctions one has to make is
between knowledge and knowing. Knowledge is cheap and
easy: knowing is costly, risky, needs courage. Knowledge is
available in the market. There are special markets for knowledge
– the universities, the colleges. Knowing is not available anywhere
except within yourself.

Knowing is your capacity. Knowledge is your memory, and
memory is a function of the mind that can be easily done by any
computer. Knowledge is always borrowed. It is not a flower that
grows in your soul, it is something plastic that has been imposed
upon you. Knowledge has no roots; it does not grow. It is a dead
compilation of corpses. Knowing is a continuous growth, it is a living
process. In other words, knowing belongs to your consciousness and
its evolution, knowledge belongs to your mind and its memory system.

The words look similar, hence they have created much confu-
sion in the world. And knowledge is cheap: you can get it from

books, you can get it from the rabbis, you can get it from the pundits, you can get it from the bishops; there are thousands of ways of accumulating knowledge. But it is a dead pile; it has no life of its own. And the most significant thing to remember is that all your knowledge, however great, makes no difference to your ignorance. Your ignorance remains intact. The only difference it makes is, it covers up your ignorance. You can pretend to the world that you are no longer ignorant, but deep inside you there is just darkness. Behind the borrowed words there is no experience.

Knowing dispels your ignorance; knowing is just like light which dispels darkness. Hence, remember the difference between the scholar and the wise man. The wise man is not necessarily a scholar and vice versa – the scholar is also not necessarily a wise man.

Most probably the scholar rarely becomes a wise man, for the simple reason that he has so much knowledge that he can deceive people, and if he can deceive many people he is deceived by their deception. He starts believing: "If so many people think me a wise man, then I must be. So many people cannot be so foolish." Hence, in the life of the scholar there is no journey, no exploration, no discovery. He lives in the greatest illusion in the world – he knows nothing and he thinks he knows all.

The man of knowing starts by disowning knowledge because knowledge is a hindrance; it is a false coin. And the false should be removed before the real can be realized. He disowns everything that is not his own. It is better to be ignorant than to be knowledgeable because at least the ignorance is yours. It needs more courage than renouncing riches, renouncing kingdoms, renouncing your family, renouncing the society because they are all outside. Knowledge accumulates inside your mind. Wherever you go, deep in the Himalayas it will be with you.

Renouncing knowledge means a deep inner cleansing and that is what I mean by meditation. Meditation is nothing but renouncing borrowed knowledge and becoming fully aware of one's ignorance. This brings a metamorphosis. The moment you are aware of your ignorance, ignorance goes through such a great change that unless it happens it remains unbelievable. The very ignorance becomes your innocence. The wise man also says, "I do not know."

According to Zarathustra, the highest stage of consciousness is that of a child. You are born a child but then you are ignorant. You will go through much knowledge, much memory and if you are fortunate enough, one day you will see that it is all false because it is not yours.

Buddha may have known, Jesus may have known, Krishna may have known; but their knowledge cannot become my knowing, their life cannot become my life, their love cannot become my love. How can their knowledge become my knowledge? I will have to seek and search on my own. I have to become an adventurer, a seeker of the unknown. I have to go on untrodden paths into uncharted seas. And I have to risk everything with a determined will that if others have achieved the truth, there is no reason why existence will be unkind to me.

Very few fortunate people start dropping their borrowed knowledge. And as they start dropping their borrowed knowledge the circle starts moving back toward their childhood. The completion of the circle comes when ignorance becomes luminous. When ignorance meets with awareness, the greatest explosion in the whole experience of man happens: you disappear as an ego. Now you are a pure innocent existence – pure isness; with no claim for anything.

In this moment Socrates said, "I do not know anything." In the same state Bodhidharma declared, "I know nothing. And moreover, my 'I' is just a linguistic convenience. Inside me there is no entity which can say 'I.' I am just using it because without it you will not be able to understand. The reality is that I have disappeared and there is only a pure sky, a pure isness – utterly innocent, with no clouds of knowledge."

It is a difficult task to disown knowledge because knowledge gives you respectability, makes you a great man, brings you a Nobel Prize. You are known to millions of people, although you know nothing about yourself. It is a very strange state: the whole world knows you except yourself. To disown knowledge means to fall in the eyes of people, to lose respectability, fame, celebrity. And the ego is very much against doing such a thing because with the respectability, the fame, and the knowledge disowned, the ego starts dying. It can live only on the borrowed. It itself is the most false thing in your life.

Zarathustra's statements have to be contemplated very deeply:

...I have left the house of scholars and slammed the door behind me.

It is not only that he has left the house – the emphasis, it should be remembered, is that he has slammed the door behind him. He is finished with scholarship. This is not the place where truth is found. This is the place where truth is discussed, this is the place where thousands of hypotheses about truth are produced, this is the place where no conclusion has ever been arrived at.

For thousands of years scholars have been discussing, in minute detail, but there has never been a conclusion. Scholars are empty shells – they make much noise but that noise is meaningless. They argue much but the hypothesis they are arguing about still remains a hypothesis; no argument can make a hypothesis a reality. And above all, how can you discuss something which you have never experienced?

The scholars are like the five blind people of Aesop's fable who had gone to see an elephant. Obviously they had no eyes. They could not see the elephant, so they touched it. Somebody touched his feet, somebody touched his big ears, somebody touched some other part, and everybody declared, "I know now what an elephant is." The one who had touched his legs said, "An elephant is just like a pillar." And the one who had touched his ears said, "You are an idiot, my experience shows that an elephant is just like a big fan." And so on and so forth. They cannot come to any conclusion. And what they are saying looks absurd: the elephant is not like a pillar, but something in the elephant is like a pillar – his legs. But at least they have touched some part of the elephant.

Scholars are in an even worse condition. They have not touched anything about truth, about love, about silence, about meditation, about ecstasy – not even a partial experience – and they are so prolific in their arguments. They create much noise; they shout at each other. For centuries they have been doing that.

Zarathustra says: *I have left the house of scholars...* It is a mad place – people are talking about things they know nothing about. Blind people are discussing detailed information about light, about darkness, about colors. People who don't have any ears are talking about music. People who have never known a single moment of silence are creating great philosophical systems based on silence. They are very articulate about words, language, grammar, but that is not the search of Zarathustra.

He slammed the door behind him, forever. Scholarship, knowledgeability is not his way, is no one's way; it is only for fools to deceive themselves.

Too long did my soul sit hungry at their table; I have not been
schooled, as they have, to crack knowledge as one cracks nuts.
I love freedom and the air over fresh soil; I would sleep on ox-skins
rather than on their dignities and respectabilities.
I am too hot and scorched by my own thought: it is often about to
take my breath away. Then I have to get into the open air and
away from all dusty rooms.
But they sit cool in the cool shade: they want to be mere spectators
in everything and they take care not to sit where the sun burns
upon the steps.

The scholar lives comfortably in his invented hypotheses, in his borrowed knowledge, in his respectability. He has no longing to experience life on his own. He loves comfort and respectability too much, which for a real seeker does not mean anything. What can respectability be – respectability from the people who are ignorant, who know nothing? They respect you, thinking that you are wise – you can quote scriptures. But the very idea of being respected by the ignorant is against the pride of an authentic man.

Comfort is a slow death. Soon death will be knocking on your doors; then neither comfort can save you, nor respectability can be a shield. The only thing that can save you is your own realization of truth, is your own knowing of the meaning of life. It is your own taste.

But the scholars don't have courage enough to drop all comfort, all respectability, and to declare to the world, "I am not a wise man, not yet. Now I am going to search, and I will stake everything to have even a glimpse of the beauty and ecstasy of reality. I have lived too much in words, now I want actual experience."

And actual experience is wordless. It is a taste, it is a nourishment, it fulfills you. The word *love* is not love. Love is a deep dance of your heart, a rejoicing in your soul, an overflowing of your life juices, a sharing with those who are receptive and available. But the word *love* has nothing to do with it.

When they give themselves out as wise, their little sayings and
truths make me shiver: their wisdom often smells as if it came from
the swamp.

It smells, it stinks, it is really disgusting. If you have known something on your own, then you can see that the so-called scholars are all carrying corpses. And they are bragging whose corpse is the most ancient. The more rotten a corpse is, the more ancient a scripture is, the greater is the scholar.

Scholars certainly stink. But the innocent man – who is no longer burdened with dusty books, who is no longer living in dusty rooms of scholarship, who has come into the open, under the sky – has a fragrance around him. Innocence has a fragrance, just as knowledge has a disgusting smell because knowledge comes from corpses, and knowing comes from a living life source.

They are clever, they have cunning fingers: what is my simplicity compared with their diversity?

Zarathustra says, "I am just a simple man, I am not clever – no wise man is clever." Cleverness is a poor substitute for wisdom; cunningness is even a perversion. The innocent man is neither clever, nor cunning; but there is tremendous beauty and grandeur in him.

I used to know a very rare human being, an old man, Magga Baba. This statement of Zarathustra's reminds me of him. Nobody knew his name. He had nothing except a jug; and the Hindi word for jug is *magga*. Because he had a jug to drink water out of, or to have food in – that was his only possession – people started calling him Magga Baba. He was so simple that people would drop money into his *magga* – he would never beg – and some other people might take money out of his *magga*, but he would never prevent it. It was none of his concern.

You will not believe me; perhaps he was the only man who was stolen many times. A man! – and he did not prevent it. People would simply take him and put him in a rickshaw. And he would not say, "Where are you taking me? And why are you taking me?" – he would simply go. They would take him to another village. And when, in the place where he was living, they became aware that somebody had stolen Magga Baba, they would go in search of him, to bring him back. He would not say anything to them either; they just had to put him back into a car or into a rickshaw.

Once he was lost for almost twelve years because some people took him far away in a train. His followers went around the villages, but he was not found because he was thousands of miles away. It was just by chance – a businessman had gone to that place and he saw Magga Baba. He dropped his business, took hold of Magga Baba, put him onto a train and brought him back to the city. There was great rejoicing all over the city: Magga Baba has been found. Twelve years! People had almost forgotten him.

He was so simple, just like a child. He used to speak very rarely – just a word, and that too not in response to your questions or anything. Once he told me, when he was alone... He used to live in a shed, an open shed, and at night his disciples used to massage him. The whole night the massage used to go on. He told me, "I need to sleep also, and these disciples of mine, they don't understand that if they continue massaging me..." And not only one – five, six people were massaging him. Somebody was massaging his head, somebody was massaging his feet.

He said, "How can I sleep? I have not slept for almost twenty years because these lovers won't let me."

I was always concerned about it, that this stupidity should be stopped, so I told the owner of the shed, "Put some doors on the shed because this is too much for the poor man. The whole day people are there and the whole night they are there – and this they call 'serving the master.' There is always a crowd serving the master, and nobody is at all concerned that he needs some rest. Put some doors on, close it at ten o'clock at night and open it in the morning."

He said, "I have been thinking about it."

I said, "There is no question of thinking, it is a simple thing."

So he managed to put the doors on. But by the time he had fixed the doors, Magga Baba had been stolen. His disciples, seeing that doors are being put on, had taken him away to another shed.

I told him, "It seems impossible, in this life, for you to sleep. I can ask again, the owner of this shed, but your disciples will take you away again. Their concern is to serve you. You don't speak..." Nobody ever asked him what he liked to eat; whatever they brought he would eat. One day I saw that he was smoking two cigarettes.

I said, "Magga Baba!"

He said, "What to do? Two disciples..."

"But," I said, "Do you smoke?"

He said, "I don't know, but they have put the cigarettes in my mouth, so what else can I do? I'm smoking – I have never smoked before. Just a competition between two disciples." Such a simplicity.

Zarathustra must have been a very simple man because his insights prove that. Only a very simple heart, utterly innocent, is capable of knowing the depths of life, and the heights of consciousness, and the mysteries of existence. Innocence is a door that leads you into all the mysteries and all the secrets of life.

Their fingers *understand all threading and knitting and weaving: thus they weave the stockings of the spirit!....*
They keep a sharp eye upon one another and do not trust one another as well as they might. Inventive in small slynesses, they lie in wait for those whose wills go upon lame feet – they lie in wait like spiders....
They also know how to play with loaded dice; and I found them playing so zealously that they were sweating.
We are strangers to one another, and their virtues are even more opposed to my taste than are their falsehoods and loaded dice.

All these things he is saying about the scholars, about the people who are recognized in the world as great men. All the mystics are strangers to the scholars, for the simple reason that the mystic does not believe, the mystic does not think; the mystic experiences. To think about water is one thing... You can write a treatise on water, and you will be known as a great scholar; you may be awarded a PhD on your thesis. But your book or your knowledge cannot quench the thirst; and the man who drinks water need not know that its chemical formula is H_2O – because "H_2O" cannot quench your thirst.

The mystic's concern is to quench his thirst, to nourish his being, to explore his interiority and to come into rapport with existence and all that it contains. And it contains all the joys, and all the beauties, and all the blessings, and all the benedictions. The scholar is content only to think about these things. He is not really thirsty; otherwise he would seek water, not a treatise on water; he would go to the well, not to the library. The mystic goes to the well and the scholar goes to the library. They are absolute strangers to each other.

We are strangers to one another, and their virtues are even more opposed to my taste than are their falsehoods and loaded dice. The scholar cannot speak the truth because he knows nothing about it. Even people who know about it cannot speak it, but at least they can point toward it; they can give a few hints, a few guidelines. They can hold your hand and take you to the window to show you the open sky and the stars. But the scholar is too much involved in language, in theology, in philosophy – he has no time even to look out of the window. He has forgotten living; he knows only thinking.

Thinking is a falsehood because you think only when you do not know. When you see a beautiful sunset, do you think? Most probably, out of old habit, you start thinking. You start saying within yourself, "What a beautiful sunset." But your words are becoming a barrier. That is not a way to be in rapport with the sunset; all thinking should stop. Then you will be there – utterly in harmony with the sunset, almost a part of it. And then you will know its beauty. Not by repeating, "It is beautiful" – those words are borrowed. You have heard them, and you are saying them just to show that you have a great aesthetic sense.

But *you* are not there; your mind is wandering somewhere else. If beauty cannot stop your mind, you don't know what beauty is. If a great dance cannot bring meditation to you, then you don't know how to see a dance. We are loaded with falsehoods.

Zarathustra says: *...their virtues are even more opposed to my taste...* Their virtues are very strange. Different scholars have different virtues, belonging to different herds. I will tell you one incident in the life of a great philosopher that India has produced – Shankaracharya, the first Adi Shankaracharya, because now there are successors, like the popes, they are all called *shankaracharyas.* He preached the philosophy that the world is illusory, that it only appears it does not exist. It is almost made of the same stuff as dreams are made of...

In Varanasi, which is the Hindu citadel, he was delivering discourses on the illusoriness of the world. One morning – it was dark, there was still time before the sun would rise... He was a brahmin monk and, according to the tradition, he took a bath in the Ganges. He was coming up the steps, there was nobody around, and suddenly a man appeared and, touching his body, passed by his side. The man then stopped and said, "Forgive me, perhaps in the darkness you cannot recognize me, but I can recognize you: I am a sudra, I am an untouchable."

Hindus have the oldest fascist religion. They have reduced

one-fourth of their society to an almost animal existence. They call them untouchables because to touch them, or even to be touched by their shadow, defiles you. You have to take a bath immediately to cleanse yourself. For five thousand years they have been torturing these poor people, who do all the dirty work of the society. They are not allowed to live in the cities, in the towns; they have to live outside. They are the poorest of the poor, the most exploited, the most downtrodden.

Shankaracharya was a high-caste brahmin, and one of the greatest Hindu philosophers. He was really very angry. He said, "You are an untouchable and you recognized me, and still you touched me. I will have to go back to the river and take another bath."

But the untouchable said, "Before you go, you will have to answer a few questions; otherwise I will remain here and touch you again."

There was nobody there, so Shankaracharya was in a fix – what to do? If he goes and takes a bath and comes back and he is touched again, the situation will be the same. So he said, "Okay, what are your questions? You seem to be a very nasty and stubborn person."

He said, "My first question is: Am I real or illusory? If I am an illusion, you need not have another bath; you can go and do your worship in the temple. If I am real, then drop this nonsense that you have been talking."

Shankara was silent for a moment – what to say to this man? He had been discussing his philosophy all over the country. He had conquered all the Hindu philosophers. A book exists, *Shankara Digvijaya*, the victory of the great Shankara. Wherever he went, he logically proved that the world is illusory. But what to do with this untouchable?

He was standing there. The untouchable said, "I am illusory, the river is illusory, your bath is illusory, you are illusory – this is all according to your philosophy. I want to ask a few things more: you call me untouchable. Is it my body that is untouchable? Do you think your body is made with different ingredients? Is it possible to find a difference between the bones of an untouchable and the bones of a brahmin, or the blood, or the skin, or the skull? I can bring skulls and you tell me which one is the skull of a brahmin. Certainly bodies are all made of the same ingredients; you cannot find any difference of superior or inferior.

"Then perhaps, our minds are untouchable. But can you touch

my mind? That which cannot be touched should not be called untouchable. Your mind is also untouchable. Or do you think my soul is untouchable? – because I have heard you speaking, that there is only one soul in the whole universe, the *brahman*, the ultimate soul, and we are all parts of it. What about the untouchables? Do they have souls or not? And if they have souls, are they part of your ultimate one soul, or do they have a separate, out-of-this-town place?"

Shankara, who was a great logician, for the first time felt defeated. He said, "Forgive me, you have awakened me from a deep sleep. I was living in words; you challenged me by reality."

The people who become accustomed to living in words start living in castles in the air. They forget the real world, the real beings. Their virtues, their religions are derived from their air castles. Their virtues are not derived from the reality in which they exist. That's why Zarathustra says: *...their virtues are even more opposed to my taste...*

They are just verbal, logical, linguistic; they have nothing to do with reality. And you can make anything a virtue – you just have to give arguments for it.

It happened to a man...

He was always coming late to his house, and his wife was continually telling him, "I know where you go and someday you will repent." But he did not listen – he was going to the prostitutes.

That night the wife was really angry, and as he entered the house she cut his nose off with a knife. The man said, "What are you doing?" But by that time his nose was on the ground. The man said, "Are you mad or something? Now, how will I live? What will I say to people?"

The woman said, "Now it is your problem. I have lived enough in anguish, now you live..."

The man thought: it is really a very embarrassing situation. Everybody in the town will be asking, "What happened to your nose?" It is better to escape from this town. But the problem still remains that in the other town they will also ask, "What happened to your nose?"

He was a man who had some interest in philosophy and religion.

He found a way: he escaped in the night to the other town, and there he sat under a tree in a lotus posture with closed eyes. People came around. They had seen many saints, but this was a special saint – without a nose and sitting absolutely buddhalike.

Finally somebody asked, "You are new here and we are happy to have a great saint like you" – because he was sitting so still, so silently; although inside there was nothing of the silence, it was just a posture.

He said, "I have found God."

They said, "You have found God? Then we would like to be your disciples."

He said, "There is a condition: unless you cut off your nose… It is the nose that is the barrier. Once the nose is cut off, immediately you will see God standing before you."

It was a difficult thing. People thought many times… But everywhere you can find idiots. Some idiot came out and he said, "Okay! I am ready."

The man had brought a knife with him. He took him aside and cut his nose off. The man looked around, but there was no God. He said, "But where is God?"

The master said, "Don't talk about God because there is no God and it has nothing to do with cutting your nose off. But if you say to people that you are not seeing God, they will laugh at you – that you are an idiot, you lost your nose unnecessarily. It is better that you just go and tell people – go dancing – that, 'This is a simple method, great. The moment the nose came off, God was standing before me.'" The man thought, and he also was convinced that this is the only way to save himself from embarrassment.

The master said, "This is the situation, the same situation with me. I don't know anything about God, but you are my chief disciple, and we will make many disciples – just have a little courage."

So the man went and told people, "I had done everything and I had not found God. This man has found the right key: just a small sacrifice of the nose and immediately it is as if a curtain has opened and God is standing there. I have seen him," and he was dancing.

People said, "This is something. We have never heard… There is no scripture in which it is written: cut your nose off and see God."

But that man was from their own village. He sat by his master's side in a lotus posture, and the line started growing. The trick was the same: he would take them to the side, cut their nose off, and tell them the fact, "There is no question of God, it is a question now of saving yourself from embarrassment. You are free, you can tell them, but they will only call you an idiot. If you listen to me you will be worshipped like a great saint, as all my followers are being worshipped."

It became so infectious that there were hundreds of people in that town without noses; and everybody was touching their feet, inviting them to their homes for food, for clothes. The rumor even reached the king.

He was a person very deeply interested in religion. He said, "But I have never heard, never read...but so many people cannot lie. If it was only one person, that would be one thing, but from our own capital, hundreds of people have seen God. To remain without the realization of God just to save your nose does not seem to be right. I'm going!"

He told the prime minister, "Make arrangements. I'm going. One day one has to die – nose and all – so if just by cutting your nose off you can experience God, it is worth it."

The prime minister was a very intelligent man. He said, "Just wait. There is no hurry. You can cut your nose off tomorrow. Let me first inquire, find out what is happening."

He went, invited the "great master" – because now he had become a great master, who had found the shortest way to God. You cannot even imagine that there can be a shorter way. He invited him into the palace and the master was very happy; he went to the palace. He was taken into a room where four very strong wrestlers were ready; he could not see what was going on.

The prime minister said, "Tell the truth; otherwise these four people are going to beat you, torture you, make as many fractures in your body as possible until you tell the truth."

The man saw the situation. He said, "The reality is, my wife has cut my nose off. I have not seen any God or anything. Please don't torture me; I will leave the city."

And the prime minister asked, "What about your other disciples?"

He said, "Nobody has seen...but once somebody's nose is gone, he has two alternatives: either to be a saint or to be a fool. The whole city will laugh, that this idiot has lost his nose and we were telling him, 'Don't do this,' but he didn't listen."

He took the man to the king, and when the king heard it he said, "My God! If I had gone yesterday, by this time I would also have seen God!"

You can find any kind of stupidity and support it by cunning-ness, by cleverness, and the world is so full of idiots that you will always find followers. All these religions that exist are nothing but different versions of the same story. Nobody has seen God, but by torturing yourself you become a saint. And then it looks foolish to say that this torturing has been useless; I have not seen God. Now it is better to keep quiet. You have become so respectable – God or no God. You were of no use, worthless, nobody ever respected you; now thousands of people respect you. It is better to keep quiet and enjoy the respectability.

Logic, argument, philosophy, in the hands of cunning and clever people, can create all kinds of virtues and moralities in which you cannot see what is moral. But they can give evidence, and they can always bring witnesses to say, "Yes. It is happening."

Hindu monks use a wooden sandal. It is very torturous because it has no support – you have to hold it between your big toe and your second toe. It is heavy and walking becomes unnecessary tor-ture. But ask the Hindu monks, "Why are you doing it when more comfortable, convenient sandals are possible?"

One great Hindu saint, Karpatri, told me that there is a secret in it. I said, "What is the secret?"

He said, "The secret is that it keeps a man celibate."

I said, "Great! The wooden sandal?"

He said, "You don't understand. There is a nerve in your big toe that controls your sexuality."

I said, "Now, man's whole physiology has been completely explored – there is no nerve there which controls sexuality. You can even cut the whole leg off, then too sexuality will not be controlled." But millions of Hindu monks believe in it. And there is another thing: every Hindu wears a sacred thread around his neck; and when he goes to the urinal, he has to put that thread around his ear.

I asked the Shankaracharya of Dwarika – I was staying in Dwarika – "I don't see the point." I had to ask him because he him-self had made a man look so foolish amongst the people. A young man had stood up and he wanted to ask something, but the Shankaracharya said, "Before you ask anything, answer my few questions." The man was wearing Western dress – long pants, a coat, and a tie – and that had infuriated the Shankaracharya.

He asked, "Do you have the Hindu thread, the sacred thread, inside your shirt or not?"

The man said, "No, I don't have it."

The Shankaracharya was very angry, and he said, "The moment you stood up, I knew – with that kind of clothes, you must be urinating standing up and that is against Hinduism. First get a sacred thread. Change these clothes, and when you are urinating put the thread round your ear." The people laughed and the poor man looked stupid among those idiots.

I had just heard about it, so I asked him, "What is the science of your sacred thread? And in what way is it spiritual to put it around your ear while urinating?"

The same answer: that in the ear there is a nerve which controls your sexuality. So when you wind the sacred thread round and round the ear, that nerve is caught. It helps a man to remain celibate.

Millions of Hindus believe this. And it is not only Hindus – in every religion you will find the same kind of stupid ideas have been propagated for thousands of years. Nobody raises any question because nobody wants to fall apart from the crowd, lose the respect of the crowd.

And the crowd can be very nasty; it can misbehave with the person. The person may have to lose his job. Even his family will become against him; his own friends will turn their backs on him. He will become lonely in the very crowd, and condemned. But if he were doing those stupid things that the crowd believes have some spirituality in them, some virtue in them, the crowd would have been respectful.

As far as I see, to be respectable in this society means you are cunning, means you are a hypocrite. It means that just to remain respectable you are pretending many things, which you know perfectly well are just either useless or stupid or even harmful.

And when I lived among them I lived above them. They grew angry with me for that.

I know it from my own experience. I have made so many religious people angry around the world – religious heads, saints, sages – just for the simple reason that I showed them that what they understand as character, as virtue, as religion, is mostly rubbish. They don't have any answer. Their answer is anger; but anger is not an argument. It does not prove anything – in fact it disproves. If you become angry, that simply shows that you have been exposed and you don't have any evidence, any proof, any rationality in your actions.

And when I lived among them I lived above them. They grew angry with me for that.
They did not want to know that someone was walking over their heads; and so they put wood and dirt and rubbish between their heads and me.
Thus they muffled the sound of my steps: and from then on the most scholarly heard me the worst....
But I walk above their heads with my thoughts in spite of that; and even if I should walk upon my own faults, I should still be above them and their heads.
For men are not equal...

This is such a great statement. Particularly today, because communism has made it almost universally accepted that all men are equal. And it is not right at all: not even two men are equal.

Equality is a false idea. Every man is unique. He is a category in himself.

I conceive that everybody should be given equal opportunity to grow in his uniqueness, but no men are equal. Equality is our contemporary superstition – the latest and the most widely accepted, even by those who are not communists. They have also accepted it because they have not denied it.

Even the non-communists don't have the guts to say that men are not equal because they are afraid that the crowds will be angry. Crowds are very happy to know that men are equal, that you are equal to Albert Einstein, that you are equal to Bertrand Russell, that you are equal to Martin Buber, that you are equal to Jean-Paul Sartre. The masses are very happy with the idea. It is so ego fulfilling that even those who are not communists are afraid to say that men are not equal. But I am absolutely in agreement with Zarathustra: men are not equal.

...thus speaks justice. And what I desire they may not desire!

My likings are different, your likings are different; my talents are different, your talents are different; my destiny is only my destiny, your destiny is only your destiny. In fact, only cattle are equal. Man is the only being on the earth who has uniqueness. But you will create anger in them.

When I said, twenty years ago, that men are not equal, the Communist party of India passed a resolution against me, condemning me. And the president of the Communist party of India, S. A. Dange, declared that soon his son-in-law, who is a professor, is going to write a book to confute my idea that men are not equal. He has written a book against me; although there is no argument except anger, abuse and lies – but not a single argument to prove that men are equal.

Zarathustra is right: *...thus speaks justice.* I have my own conception of a better society: it will provide equal opportunity to all, but the equal opportunity will be for them to be unequal, to grow in their uniqueness.

To me, communism means equal opportunity for all, not equality of man. Zarathustra had the insight twenty-five centuries ago. It is absolutely just and fair that man should not be sacrificed again in the name of equality. He has been sacrificed many times, in different names, in different temples, before different gods. Now he is being sacrificed in the temple of communism – before a holy book, *Das Kapital*, before a trinity of gods, Marx, Engels and Lenin.

It is such a simple thing; everybody knows that nobody is equal. But man's jealousy – jealousy of the small man against the great, jealousy of the little ones against the giants, makes them shout loudly. And of course they are in the majority: "Man is equal, and equality is man's birthright." And they know not that they are saying something which is synonymous to committing suicide. Equal opportunity to grow is perfectly right. And the acceptance of the uniqueness of individuals makes the society rich, gives it the variety of all kinds of flowers, of different colors, with different fragrances.

Zarathustra is rare, in the sense that he has seen faraway things because nobody was talking about equality of man in his day. Marx was yet to come, after twenty-four centuries. But the more meditative you are, the more silent, the clearer becomes your vision, and it can see far away in the future. This statement is against Karl Marx; although Zarathustra is not aware of any Karl Marx in particular.

Karl Marx was just a scholar and nothing else. He spent his whole life in the library of the British Museum. He was there before the library opened, and he was almost pushed out, every day, when the library closed – and sometimes even carried out because in his old age he would continue reading and reading, and he would become unconscious. By the time the library was going to close they would find that his head was on the table and he was unconscious. He had to be carried out and an ambulance called to take him home. And tomorrow morning he was back again. A perfect scholar! Not metaphorically, but really a bookworm. All his experience was only with books – not with people, not with existence, not with himself. *For men are not equal: thus speaks justice. And what I desire they may not desire!*

...Thus spake Zarathustra.

CHAPTER 7

rebellion is the only hope

Of Redemption

Truly, my friends, I walk among men as among the fragments and limbs of men!

The terrible thing to my eye is to find men shattered in pieces and scattered as if over a battlefield of slaughter.

And when my eye flees from the present to the past, it always discovers the same thing: fragments and limbs and dreadful chances – but no men!

The present and the past upon the earth – alas! my friends – that is my most intolerable burden; and I should not know how to live, if I were not a seer of that which must come.

A seer, a willer, a creator, a future itself and a bridge to the future – and alas, also like a cripple upon this bridge: Zarathustra is all this.

And even you have often asked yourselves: Who is Zarathustra to us? What shall we call him? and, like me, you answer your own questions with questions.

Is he a promiser? Or a fulfiller? A conqueror? Or an inheritor? A harvest? Or a plowshare? A physician? Or a convalescent?

Is he a poet? Or a genuine man? A liberator? Or a subduer? A good man? Or an evil man?...
And it is all my art and aim, to compose into one and bring together what is fragment and riddle and dreadful chance....
Will – that is what the liberator and bringer of joy is called: thus I have taught you, my friends! But now learn this as well: The will itself is still a prisoner.
Willing liberates: but what is it that fastens in fetters even the liberator?
"It was": that is what the will's teeth-gnashing and most lonely affliction is called. Powerless against that which has been done, the will is an angry spectator of all things past.
The will cannot will backwards; that it cannot break time and time's desire – that is the will's most lonely affliction.
Willing liberates: what does willing itself devise to free itself from its affliction and to mock at its dungeon?...
The spirit of revenge: my friends, that, up to now, has been mankind's chief concern; and where there was suffering, there was always supposed to be punishment.
"Punishment" is what revenge calls itself: it feigns a good conscience for itself with a lie....
"Except the will at last redeem itself and willing become not-willing –": but you, my brothers, know this fable-song of madness! I led you away from these fable-songs when I taught you: "The will is a creator...."
Has the will become its own redeemer and bringer of joy? Has it unlearned the spirit of revenge...

...Thus spake Zarathustra.

Zarathustra is absolutely clear that religions have destroyed man's integrity. They have broken him – not only in parts, but into opposing parts. The greatest crime against humanity has been committed by the religions. They have made humanity schizophrenic; they have given everybody a split personality. It has been done in a very clever and cunning way.

First, man has been told, "You are not the body," and second, "The body is your enemy." And this was the logical conclusion – that you are not part of the world, and the world is nothing but your punishment; you are here to be punished. Your life is not, and cannot be, a rejoicing; it can only be a mourning, it can only be a tragedy. Suffering is going to be your lot on the earth.

They had to do it in order to praise God, who is a poetic fiction; and to praise heaven, which is an extension of human greed. And to make people afraid of hell, which is to create a great fear in the very center of the human soul. This way they have taken away man and dissected him.

No religion accepts the simple, natural and factual phenomenon that man is a unity and this world is not a punishment. And this world is not separate from man. Man is rooted in this world just as trees are rooted. This planet, the earth, is his mother.

Zarathustra has repeated again and again, "Never betray the earth." All the religions have betrayed the earth. They have betrayed their own mother, they have betrayed their own life source. They have condemned the earth, and they have argued for renouncing it – renunciation is their continual emphasis.

But how can you renounce your nature? You can pretend, you can be a hypocrite. You can even start believing that you are no longer part of nature; but even your greatest saints depend on nature, just as your greatest sinners do. They need food, they need water, they need air; their needs don't change. What is their renunciation?

It creates a split mind within them. They fall apart into fragments, and these fragments are continuously fighting with each other. This is the root cause of human misery, and it has become almost an established thing because people have been suffering for thousands of years. Now they have started taking it for granted: "This is our lot, this is our fate, this is our destiny. Nothing can be done about it." The reality is, it is neither our fate nor our destiny. It is our stupidity, it is our unintelligence that we have been listening to the priests, believing in their fictions.

Of course, those fictions are very profitable to the priests. They have not bothered to butcher humanity into fragments because these fictions serve their interests perfectly well. A healthy and whole man, a man who is not divided into fragments, cannot be enslaved by the priests. Only a man who is suffering needs prayer – in the hope that perhaps God may help him. For God to exist, man has to suffer. To make God more and more a reality, man has to become more and more schizophrenic.

The more man is in pain, the more easily he can be convinced to pray, to do religious rituals because he wants to get rid of the pain. He can be convinced about the saviors, messengers of God, prophets. But a man who is living blissfully, living a life of joy, does not need any God. A man who is living life does not need any prayer. It is the sickness of man's mind that is absolutely needed for the priests and their profession.

Zarathustra is not a priest. He is perhaps one of the first psychologists to have discovered the schizophrenic state of the human mind.

He says:

Truly, my friends, I walk among men as among the fragments and limbs of men!

It is so difficult to find a man who is whole; everybody is just a fragment. Somebody is spiritual, he denies his body; somebody is materialist, he denies his soul. The spiritualist not only denies the body, he also denies the mind.

All theologies are very jealous and very monopolistic. In America, at the end of the last century, there was a great religious movement called Christian Science. They believed only in the soul. Everything else is just an illusion – just your thought, there is no reality in it. They had their own churches where they used to meet to discuss their great philosophy.

A young man met an old woman on the street one day, and the old woman said, "What happened to your father? – because he is not coming to our meetings anymore."

The young man said, "He has been sick."

The woman laughed. She said, "Sickness is just a thought. He thinks he is sick; otherwise how can the soul be sick? Tell him that this is not right for a Christian Scientist."

After two, three weeks again she encountered the young man, and she asked, "What happened? He is still not coming to the meetings."

The young man said, "Lady, what can I do? Now he thinks he is dead! We tried to convince him, 'It is only your thought, you are not dead,' but he does not listen. We reminded him, 'You are a Christian Scientist, it is not right for you to believe in a thought. Start breathing!' But he believes in his thought so much that we had to take him to the graveyard. There was no way…"

There are people who are denying even the existence of the body. There are people who are denying even the existence of the mind. And there are also people who are denying the existence of the soul; they say only the body is real and all else is fiction. All these people – spiritualists, materialists – are agreed on one point: that they will not leave man natural, one organic unity; something has to be discarded. But that which you discard hangs around you; it is part of you. You can, by constant repetition – repetition of centuries – make yourself believe. But if your belief is not according to nature, suffering will be the result.

The whole of humanity is suffering. And the amazing phenomenon is that the suffering of humanity is because of these religious ideas, which do not allow man to grow naturally, to live naturally, to love naturally. And then when suffering comes, they say, "Look! Have we not been telling you that this earth is nothing but a punishment?"

It is a very cunning strategy. First you create suffering, and then you use suffering as an argument to support the idea that you are born in sin, and your being on the earth and not in paradise is a punishment.

Because Adam and Eve disobeyed God, you are suffering. It is a strange logic. Even if Adam and Eve had disobeyed God, it was not such a great sin – they had only eaten one apple. Because of their eating the apple – and we don't know whether Adam and Eve ever existed or not – thousands of years afterward you are suffering because you are carrying their heritage. You belong to the line, and your originators were sinners; hence you are also sinners. And the suffering of life proves it; otherwise, why is there so much suffering?

Religions have been very cunning, priests have been very inhuman. They have divided man against himself; fighting with himself he suffers.

Zarathustra is right: *Truly, my friends, I walk among men as among fragments and limbs of men!* It is very difficult to find a total man. The total man will be the superman, the total man will be the happiest man, the total man will have all the blessings this beautiful planet can shower on him. But only the total man can have it.

Why can the total man be blissful? – because the total man lives totally, lives intensely; each moment he squeezes the juice of life. His life is a dance, his life is a celebration.

And suddenly, when your life is a celebration, you cannot believe that it is a punishment. Then you can see through the lies of the priests, and then you don't need any paradise because you have it already here and now. You don't have to postpone it far away, after your death.

The terrible thing to my eye is to find men shattered in pieces and scattered as if over a battlefield of slaughter.

Zarathustra sees things very clearly, with a clarity which is rare. What we call humanity he sees as: ...*a battlefield of slaughter.*

Everybody has been destroyed in some way or other, everybody has been stopped from growing. Everybody is missing something which is absolutely needed, and which was his birthright to have. The condemners – and all the priests are condemners – cannot see anybody happy, anybody joyous; they immediately turn upon him and start condemning his joy, condemning his pleasure. And they have developed great arguments about how to destroy people's pleasure.

Their greatest argument is that this life is very small, and pleasure is very ephemeral, continuously changing. Don't be deceived by it because if you are deceived by it you will miss the eternal blissfulness of paradise.

Naturally, the stake is very big. Just for the small pleasure of enjoying your morning tea, you would not like to destroy your eternal blissfulness in paradise. And this life consists of small pleasures; but if all those pleasures are put together, your life becomes a pleasure unto itself. One does not need big pleasures. And their paradise and its eternal blissfulness is only poetry because nobody has ever seen it. Nobody has come back and said, "Yes, I am an eyewitness."

In the name of fictitious gods, and in the name of fictitious pleasures, what is real has been destroyed.

And when my eye flees from the present to the past, it always discovers the same thing: fragments and limbs of dreadful chances – but no men!
The present and the past upon the earth – alas! my friends – this is

*my most intolerable burden; and I should not know how to live, if I
were not a seer of that which must come.*

Zarathustra is saying, "Looking at the past of humanity and the
present is so painful, is such an agony, that I would never have
thought I could survive it. The pain is too much; it would have broken
my heart. The only thing that is keeping me alive is the hope that
there is still a future. The past is finished. The present is becoming the
past every moment. But there is still a hope that man may become
free from the chains of religion, that man may see how he has been
cheated, deceived, exploited, and in that seeing will arise the total
man, the superman.

"Just the hope of the superman is keeping me alive. Otherwise
looking at the past and the present is such a burden, is so depressing,
that I would have died of the depression."

And Zarathustra is right. It is only the hope that one day man
will understand – how long can he remain in the prisons created
by the priests? They may call them churches and temples and
mosques; it does not matter what names they give to their prisons. It
is so painful to see human beings labeled like cattle: somebody is a
Hindu, somebody is a Mohammedan, somebody is a Christian.

Going around the earth, it is very difficult to find a single human
being who has not been stamped, who is still free from the mob,
who is still free from the crowd, who is still himself, who is one single
whole, and who is living fearlessly according to his nature.

Except nature there is no religion. And you don't have to learn
what nature is. When you feel thirsty, you know you need water.
When you feel hungry, you know you need food. Your nature continuously guides you. Except nature there is no other guide. All other
guides are misguides. They take you away from the natural course,
and once you are out of your natural course, misery starts. And your
misery is their joy because only the miserable go to the churches,
only the miserable go to the temples.

When you are feeling happy and joyous, young and healthy,
who cares about the churches? Life is so rich, and life is such a
joy, who wants to enter those graveyards where sadness is thought
to be seriousness? Where a long face is thought to be religious?
Where to burst into laughter you will be condemned as a mad-
man? Where dancing is not allowed? Where love is prohibited?

Where you have to sit listening to dead words, so old and so dusty they don't touch your heart, they don't give a thrill to your being? But these churches and temples and mosques have dominated man.

Zarathustra hopes, just like every mystic, that this cannot go on forever. Someday the intelligence of man is going to rebel.

Rebellion is the only hope. Someday man is going to destroy all these so-called houses of God because this planet, this sky full of stars, is the only temple there is; all other temples are man-made. And this life in the trees, in the animals, in human beings is the only living God.

The gods that are sitting in the temples are just manufactured by man. It is very strange that these religions go on saying that God created the world, but their gods are created by men. They say, "God created the human being just like himself. He created man in his own image."

The truth is just the contrary – man has created God in his own image. That's why a Chinese god will be different from a Hindu god, an African god will be different from a European god – because people are creating gods in their own image. And the stupidity reaches to its extreme: you create those images and then you kneel down before them. Can you think of anything more idiotic? And then you start praying.

Children could be forgiven; they love their toys and they love their teddy bears. But you have not grown up, you also love your teddy bears. Your teddy bears are in your temples, in your churches, in your synagogues. But they are teddy bears – they fulfill the same function.

The child feels alone without the teddy bear. A small child was here a few days ago. His mother is a sannyasin, Amrito from Greece, and when I was in Greece he became very friendly with me. He brought a teddy bear for me! And he told his mother, "I will not leave India unless I give the teddy bear to Osho because he lives alone, he needs some companions."

What are your gods? Consolations because you feel, even in the crowd, that you are alone. You need a teddy bear in the sky, an eternal teddy bear who will be always with you. He is omniscient, omnipresent, omnipotent – he can do anything. He is just a consolation. The people who believe in God have not allowed themselves to be grown-ups. They have remained retarded in their psychology; otherwise there would be no need of any God.

Life is enough unto itself. And it is so beautiful, so full of songs and flowers and birds on the wing – it is absolute freedom to grow and to be yourself. It does not give you ten commandments, it accepts you as you are. It does not make much fuss about how you should be; its love and respect for all that is living is unconditional.

For what do you need your gods? – because you are miserable. So this is the strategy: don't let people become happy, otherwise, religion will disappear.

In one of his great insights, Bertrand Russell has said, "If the whole world becomes happy, I can guarantee there will be no religions anymore." And what he is saying has tremendous truth in it. Religions want people to remain poor, to remain sick, to remain miserable, to remain always in anxiety. Then naturally they become weak, and they need some support, and the priest is ready to give the support. He is ready to inform God, "This man needs your compassion" – although no prayer seems to be heard at all.

But the priests are very clever. They say, "Your prayers are not heard because you are not worthy. You don't deserve. You are sinners. You are committing things against religion." And it is almost impossible to live without committing some sin.

In India one of the religions, Jainism, has five great principles. The first great principle is *aswad*, no taste; eat, but don't enjoy the taste. Now you are putting man in such difficult situations. He has taste buds in his tongue – unless he goes through plastic surgery and those taste buds are removed, he will have to taste.

When something bitter comes into your mouth you will have to taste its bitterness; and so too with the sweet. But you have done something wrong because taste is of the body: you have to fight against the body and you are enjoying the body.

They have made everything impossible for man, so everybody is unworthy. And naturally, if you are unworthy: you have desires, you have longings – all are condemned. You have a biology; you are born out of biology, your every cell is nothing but sexual energy.

You would like to love someone, but all religions are against it – love, and your hell is certain! But your biology forces you to love, so you love half-heartedly, with fear, with great sadness in the heart, knowing that you are committing a sin. Naturally, you cannot enjoy love. And because you cannot enjoy, you need more; and because you need more, you go on becoming a bigger sinner. So you can

say to anybody, without even looking into his biography, that he is
unworthy – that's why his prayer has not been heard.

The fact is, there is nobody to hear it. The fact is, there is nobody
to answer it. The fact is that the man who is praying has remained
stuck somewhere psychologically.

After the Second World War, they wanted to know the average
mental age of the soldiers because by that time psychologists had
become more efficient at measuring intelligence. They were shocked.
They had never thought that this would be the result. The average
mental age of the soldiers was thirteen years! And those soldiers are
no more unintelligent than anybody else.

So it seems the body goes on growing – growing old of course –
and the mind stops at the age of thirteen or fourteen. So you may be
eighty years old, but when you are kneeling down before a god you
are just a thirteen-year-old boy; although you are kneeling with your
body, it is also your psychology.

Religions have done much harm. Nobody has bothered about
why the mental age stops at thirteen or fourteen. It is so simple: that
is the time when the boys and girls become sexually mature. At the
time when they become sexually mature, biology needs no more
intelligence.

Unless you make an effort on your own, your mental age will
remain at fourteen, thirteen. Biology has come to its fulfillment. You
are sexually mature – this much intelligence is enough to reproduce
children. If you want more intelligence, then you have to make an
effort for it, then you have to meditate, then you have to sharpen
your intelligence.

But all the religions never want you to be intelligent because
their teaching is to believe. A believer need not have any intelligence. Unless you learn to doubt, your intelligence will not grow
because doubt means inquiry; belief means there is no question of
any inquiry.

Because of the belief systems imposed on man, his mental
age has remained at fourteen, and these fourteen-year-olds are
Christians, Hindus, Mohammedans. If their intelligence grows higher,
they will start seeing that what they used to think of as religions are
nothing but superstitions. If their intelligence goes on growing, they
will start doubting about God, about heaven, about hell; they will
start doubting about the priest and his religiousness; they will start

questioning everything. And religions don't have answers.

Just now I said to you, Jainism believes that "no taste" is one of the fundamentals of their religion. I asked one Jaina monk, "If no taste is a fundamental of your religion, then why have taste buds been given by nature to man?" Nature never gives anything unnecessarily.

The Buddhist monk has to walk looking only four feet ahead. He cannot look more than that, he cannot keep his head straight because he may see some beautiful woman – that is the problem. Looking four feet ahead, at the most he can see some woman's feet, but not the woman's face.

But if love between man and woman is something wrong, why should nature give that longing? – any intelligent person is going to ask. Even Buddha would not have been born. It is good that Buddha's father was not a Buddhist monk; otherwise we would have missed all these great people.

Nature wants to reproduce: new life, new forms, better life, better forms. Nature is a continuous process of evolution. But religions are against this because the more evolved a person is, the less is the possibility that he can become a victim of any religious stupidity.

Bertrand Russell was one of the most intelligent men of this century. He lived almost a whole century, a long life, and even at the time of his last breath he was as young and intelligent as ever. He went on growing in his intelligence. And the result was, he started doubting all kinds of stupid ideas that had been told to him in his childhood. He was born in a very orthodox time in England, in the Victorian Age; but he could write a book, *Why I Am Not a Christian.*

His book is a milestone, and it has not been answered by Christianity even now, fifty years after its publication. He has questioned every Christian concept, and made it clear: "This is simply fictitious, and only people who are retarded can believe in it."

If intelligence grows, temples will be empty, but life will become immensely beautiful.

"This is the only hope," says Zarathustra.

A seer, a willer, a creator, a future itself and a bridge to the future – and alas, also like a cripple upon this bridge: Zarathustra is all this.

He is saying, "I am living only because of the hope that the night, however long, is going to end; that the dawn will come. The dawn comes to every night. This night in which humanity is living cannot be forever."

But right now he describes his situation: *A seer...* he can see far away, *...a willer...* and he can will for the superman, *...a creator...* and he is doing everything to create the man that will succeed this humanity: *...a future itself and a bridge to the future – and alas, also like a cripple upon this bridge...*

He is saying, "I am the future because I can see it. To me, it is almost the present. I can see the dawn is not far away, and I am making every effort to bring it closer. I am a bridge between this humanity and the coming superman, but I am also crippled. I cannot be the superman. I can only be the bridge and over me will pass humanity into a new age, into a new space, into a more beautiful and more blissful existence." Zarathustra is all this.

> *And even you have often asked yourselves: Who is Zarathustra to us? What shall we call him? and, like me, you answer your own questions with questions.*
> *Is he a promiser?*

Just like others, who have promised much and delivered nothing...

> *Or a fulfiller? A conqueror? Or an inheritor? A harvest? Or a plowshare? A physician? Or a convalescent?*
> *Is he a poet? Or a genuine man? A liberator? Or a subduer? A good man? Or an evil man?...*
> *And it is all my art and aim, to compose into one and bring together what is fragment and riddle and dreadful chance.*

He says, "Just one thing to be remembered about me – I am not giving you any promise. I am not proclaiming that I am a messiah, or a messenger. All that I can say is this: *...it is all my art and aim, to compose into one and bring together what is fragment and riddle and dreadful chance.*"

I want man to be together. And this is my whole art and whole aim. I want to put together all the fragments that have been shattered, and to make men whole. I am against all divisions, all dualities, and

I want man to be just like a child, enjoying life without any fear, with wholeheartedness.

Will – that is what the liberator and bringer of joy is called: thus I have taught you, my friends! But now learn this as well: The will itself is still a prisoner.

Zarathustra has been teaching up to now, will to power. Now he goes a little farther ahead. He says, "Even will to power becomes a prison."

One becomes imprisoned in it. One has to transcend that too. First, will to power; and then relax. Forget about the will, and forget about the power, and just be a child playing on the sea beach – innocent, full of wonder, unafraid of anything, trusting existence totally. That will be your liberation.

He has divided consciousness into three stages: the camel, which is the consciousness of a slave, who wants to be burdened, who is always ready to kneel down and be loaded; the lion, that is the will to power; and the third, the child. The highest is the innocence of the child. The innocence of the child is the only thing that makes you religious.

Willing liberates: but what is it that fastens in fetters even the liberator?
"It was": that is what the will's teeth-gnashing and most lonely affliction is called. Powerless against that which has been done, the will is an angry spectator of all things past.

The will liberates, but it cannot forget the past. So even though the will to power liberates man, he remains secretly burdened with the past memories of those days of slavery and darkness. And there is no way for the will to undo the past – what has happened has happened. Nothing can be done about it. Only in the innocence of the child does the past disappear.

Have you ever observed a simple experiment? If you try to remember backward, how far can you go? Four years, three years at the most. When you were four years old, up to that point you remember things. What happens? Why can you not remember those four years? – because you have lived, and there must have been experiences.

The reason is that innocence does not collect memories. Innocence remains unscratched, nothing is written on it.

That's why you can remember the whole past, but suddenly there comes a stop and that will be either at the age of four if you are a man, or it will be the age of three if you are a woman – because girls mature sooner than boys. There is one year's difference in their maturity. Girls become sexually mature at the age of thirteen, boys become sexually mature at the age of fourteen. Boys are always lagging behind; girls are more together.

Experienced mothers know – if they have given birth to two or three children – whether they have a girl or a boy growing inside them because girls remain very quiet; even in pregnancy, those nine months they remain very silent. Boys start kicking here and there – they start playing football! It seems natural to men to be doing something or other. Just to sit silently seems to be very difficult for them; they are fidgety.

Girls are more centered. Perhaps they are closer to nature because they are going to be mothers and nature is the mother. Boys are just on the margin. It is possible for a girl to enter into meditation more easily than for a boy; naturally, they are calm and quiet. Boys are all over the place, running for no purpose. All boys are Americans – they love speed. Don't ask where they are going, just ask whether they are going with full speed or not.

If you go backward, you stop at the age of four or three. What happened to those three years? No trace is left in the memory. You were so innocent that you never collected memories. You lived each moment so totally that it never left any residue.

Memories are made by unlived moments, memories are made by incomplete experiences so they hang around you. They are asking to be completed; they become your dreams. They are continuously harassing your mind, "Something has to be done, it is still incomplete." But the innocent mind lives every moment with such completion that it leaves no marks behind. It is just like the birds flying in the sky – they don't leave their footprints.

Although the will to power liberates you, there are still chains deep in your memories.

"It was": that is what the will's teeth-gnashing and most lonely affliction is called. Powerless against that which has been done, the

will is an angry spectator of all things past.
The will cannot will backwards; that it cannot break time and
time's desire – that is the will's most lonely affliction.
Willing liberates: what does willing itself devise to free itself from its
affliction and to mock at its dungeon?...
The spirit of revenge: *my friends, that up to now, has been*
mankind's chief concern; and where there was suffering, there was
always supposed to be punishment.
"Punishment" is what revenge calls itself: it feigns a good
conscience for itself with a lie.

Somebody murders, and your courts and your law and your police are going to murder the murderer. But they will do it with a method: there will be a great trial and a great show: "Justice has to be done." But this is all nonsense. The fact is, the society wants revenge. But it wants to camouflage it in beautiful words of justice.

What kind of justice is this? One man is murdered. By sending the other man to the gallows you cannot revive the first man. By sending the second man to the gallows, instead of one murder there are two murders. This is justice!

And are you certain that this man who murdered – he still has a future, he may change. He may become a great saint. Perhaps because he has murdered; that very act may bring a transformation to his being.

You are taking away that opportunity and you call it justice. It is pure and simple revenge – one hundred percent pure revenge. But it is done with great ritual, in a beautiful temple of justice, in the court, where servants of society, paid servants of society are sitting as judges. Paid servants of society will go through a ceremonial ritual – they call it a trial – and finally the man is sent to the gallows. Nietzsche is saying that this is simply revenge.

"Punishment" is what revenge calls itself: it feigns a good
conscience for itself with a lie....
"Except the will at last redeems itself and willing become not-
willing –": but you, my brothers, know this fable-song of madness!

People will call you mad.
He is saying, "Life goes on transcending itself." The same rule

applies to willing. Will also needs to transcend itself. Willing also has to disappear into silence – only then the lion changes into a child. Many have wondered how the lion can become the child; they seem to be poles apart.

But such questions are raised by those who don't understand the dialectics of life. Only a lion can become a child because to be innocent in this cunning world needs immense courage – the courage of a lion. To be trusting in this deceiving world is not possible for a coward, it is possible only for a lion; and the child is innocent, trusting.

It is one of the secrets of life that if you can be innocent and trusting, it is very difficult to deceive you. Your very innocence, your very trust prevents the deceiver.

You may have observed it – I have observed it myself many times because I have been traveling around the country for almost twenty years, waiting for trains on the platform. If you want to go to the toilet, or you want to have a cup of tea, you strangely trust an absolutely unknown person who is sitting by your side on the bench, and you tell him, "Just look after my luggage, I will be coming back." Have you ever wondered that you don't know that man? He could take all your luggage.

But it never happens, no stranger ever deceives you. There must be some great principle behind it. Your very trusting becomes a barrier. You have trusted him, now he has to prove that he is trustworthy – although he is a stranger, there is no need to prove anything; he can simply escape with your luggage and you will never see him again. And he may be a thief, may be a criminal. You don't know who he is. But almost everybody trusts strangers on the railway platforms, "Just watch my luggage, I am coming back." And I have never heard anybody complaining that his trust has been exploited.

Trusting creates a certain energy around you which has its own protective aura. Innocence prevents people from deceiving you. It is easier to deceive a person who himself is a deceiver; it is easier to cheat a person who himself is a cheat. But someone who trusts, someone who is innocently ready to be exploited and cheated is never exploited and cheated. The very energy of innocence is a great protection. Trust functions almost like a shield. But the world will call you mad.

I led you away from these fable-songs when I taught you: "The will

is a creator...."
Has the will become its own redeemer and bringer of joy? Has it
unlearned the spirit of revenge...

Unless the will surpasses itself, it cannot forget the past. And if you cannot forget the past, you are chained to it. The last function of the will is to transcend itself, to go beyond itself.

On this point, Zarathustra is in agreement with Gautam Buddha. They have followed different paths – Buddha calls this state "desire-lessness," and Zarathustra calls it "will-lessness."

You have arrived home. There is nothing to desire, there is nothing to will. You have reached the fulfillment, the actualization of your potential. Flowers have come to your being.

...Thus spake Zarathustra.

man is a becoming

The Wanderer
Zarathustra speaks to himself:
I am a wanderer and a mountain-climber...I do not like the plains and it seems I cannot sit still for long.
And whatever may yet come to me as fate and experience – a wandering and a mountain-climbing will be in it: in the final analysis one experiences only oneself.
The time has passed when accidents could befall me; and what could still come to me that was not already my own?
It is returning, at last it is coming home to me – my own Self and those parts of it that have long been abroad and scattered among all things and accidents.
And I know one thing more: I stand now before my last summit and before the deed that has been deferred the longest. Alas, I have to climb my most difficult path! Alas, I have started upon my loneliest wandering!
But a man of my sort does not avoid such an hour: the hour that says to him: "Only now do you tread your path of greatness! Summit and abyss – they are now united in one!
"You are treading your path of greatness: now what was formerly

your ultimate danger has become your ultimate refuge!...
"You are treading your path of greatness: no one shall steal after you here! Your foot itself has extinguished the path behind you, and above that path stands written: Impossibility.
"And when all footholds disappear, you must know how to climb upon your own head: how could you climb upward otherwise?
"Upon your own head and beyond your own heart! Now the gentlest part of you must become the hardest....
"In order to see much one must learn to look away from oneself – every mountain-climber needs this hardness.
"But he who, seeking enlightenment, is over-eager with his eyes, how could he see more of a thing than its foreground!
"You, however, O Zarathustra, have wanted to behold the ground of things and their background: so you must climb above yourself – up and beyond, until you have even your stars under you!"
Yes! To look down upon myself and even upon my stars: that alone would I call my summit, that has remained for me as my ultimate summit!...
Man, however, is the most courageous animal: with his courage he has overcome every animal. With a triumphant shout he has even overcome every pain; human pain, however, is the deepest pain.
Courage also destroys giddiness at abysses: and where does man not stand at an abyss? Is seeing itself not – seeing abysses?
Courage is the best destroyer: courage also destroys pity. Pity, however, is the deepest abyss: as deeply as man looks into life, so deeply does he look also into suffering.
Courage, however, is the best destroyer, courage that attacks: it destroys even death, for it says: "Was that life? Well then! Once more!"
But there is a great triumphant shout in such a saying. He who has ears to hear, let him hear.

...Thus spake Zarathustra.

One of the most fundamental things to be understood by all those who are in search – in search of a path, in search of a direction, in search of a meaning, in search of themselves – is that they will have to become wanderers. They cannot remain static. They have to learn to be a process rather than being an event.

The greatest distinguishing mark between things and man, between animals and man, is that things remain the same; they cannot become wanderers. Animals are also born complete – they don't grow up, they only grow old. A deer is born a deer and will die a deer. There is no process between birth and death, no becoming.

Man is the only being on the earth – and perhaps in the whole universe – who can become a process, a movement, a growing. Not just growing old, but growing up to new levels of consciousness, to new stages of awareness, to new spaces of experience. And there is the possibility in man that he can even transcend himself, he can go beyond himself. That is taking the process to its logical end.

In other words, I would like you to remember that man is not to be understood as a being because the word *being* gives a wrong idea – as if man is complete.

Man is a becoming.

Man is the only animal who is not complete. And that is his glory, not his curse; it is his blessing. He can be born as a man, and he can die as a Zarathustra, or as a Gautam Buddha, or as a Jesus Christ – who have transcended humanity and reached to a new space you can call enlightenment, you can call awakening, you can call godliness, but something superhuman. Man is a becoming. Zarathustra uses the parable of the wanderer for this fundamental truth about man.

Zarathustra speaks to himself...

And naturally when somebody like Zarathustra speaks to himself he speaks more authentically, more truthfully than when he speaks to others. Speaking to others, he has to concede and compromise with the others; otherwise he will be speaking a language which is only going to be misunderstood. He has to come down from his heights to the dark valleys of those with whom he is speaking.

But when he speaks with himself he can speak on the sunlit peaks, without any compromise. He can say exactly what he wants to say because he is saying it to himself, not to anybody else; there is no problem of being misunderstood. The monologue and the dialogue are two totally different phenomena.

One of the most significant Jewish philosophers of this century, Martin Buber, has contributed the idea of the dialogue to world thought. According to him, dialogue is the most significant thing. But perhaps he does not know that monologue has a height which no dialogue can ever have. So when Zarathustra speaks to himself, listen more carefully because he is speaking from the very source of his heart – and without any compromise, without any concern that he may be understood or not understood.

He is talking to himself, and these are the most important statements that he makes.

Zarathustra speaks to himself:
I am a wanderer and a mountain-climber...I do not like the plains and it seems I cannot sit still for long.

What he is saying represents exactly the innermost longing of human beings. They are all wanderers, although they have not dared to wander and they have not dared to mountain climb. Perhaps this is one of the basic reasons why they are miserable: their greatest longing remains unfulfilled; they are tied down to the plains.

There are reasons why they are tied down to the plains – it is more comfortable, it is more convenient, it is less dangerous, more secure. But it is not according to the innermost longing of the soul. The soul wants to soar high in the skies, it wants to go into unknown lands, it wants to wander on paths that are virgin. It wants to climb mountains which have never been climbed before.

It is something essentially human; it is born with man. You can keep it repressed, but then you will remain sad, miserable, and you will always feel something is missing. You may accumulate money, you may accumulate power, you may become very respectable, but inside yourself there will remain something unfulfilled, still hankering for the stars.

Man is certainly a moon-gazer. Deep down, everybody is a lunatic. The word *lunatic* comes from *luna*, the moon. Everybody wants to reach to the moon. It is not a question of finding something there, the question is of reaching there. The very pilgrimage is the bliss – not the goal.

The goal is perhaps nothing but an excuse to wander because whenever one reaches a goal, immediately he starts preparing for a new journey, a new pilgrimage. That goal has served its purpose. All goals are just to help you to keep on moving.

Movement is such a joy because movement is life. Movement is such an ecstasy because the moment you stop moving, you are dead. You may go on breathing, but that does not mean life. Movement brings you all the songs and all the dances possible.

Rabindranath Tagore has written a very strange poem. The poem is immensely significant in understanding the wandering spirit of man.

Rabindranath says that he is in search of God. Perhaps God too is the ultimate excuse for wandering, perhaps the best excuse because you will never find him; the wandering will remain eternal. That is the beauty of God – you can long for him, but you cannot find him; nobody has ever found him. The people who deny God are not aware of the deep psychology behind the fiction of God. They don't know that if you deny God, if you deny paradise, if you deny the afterlife, you are denying movement for man.

If you deny soul, if you deny consciousness, if you say consciousness is nothing but a by-product of matter as the communists say… The way Karl Marx has defined consciousness is as a by-product of matter, nothing much. Whether he is right or wrong is not the question, the question is that if he is accepted he has destroyed your every possibility of movement. He has denied you the exploration of the unknown and the unknowable.

Rabindranath says, "I was in search of God, and once in a while I would see him far away, near a star. But by the time I would reach that star, lives would have passed and God would have moved somewhere else, and the search continued. One day, suddenly, I reached a place in front of a beautiful palace, and on the signboard it said in golden letters 'The House of God.' First I was thrilled – thrilled that I had made it after all – and I rushed up the many steps leading to the door of the palace.

"But just as I was going to knock on the door, a thought suddenly paralyzed me – my hand remained paralyzed, without knocking, near the door – a thought that 'If in reality this is the house of God and he opens the door, then I am finished. My whole joy was the search, my whole joy was looking for God. After meeting God, what am I going to do?'"

A great fear grips him. He takes his shoes off and, carrying them in his hands, goes back down the steps. He is afraid – although he has not knocked on the door, hearing the noise of the shoes, of footsteps, God himself may open the door and say, "Where are you going? I am here."

"And then I ran away from that house, faster than I had ever run before. Now I am again searching for God. I know where he lives, so I can avoid that place and go on searching all over the universe. The search continues, my adventure continues, my excitement continues, tomorrow remains meaningful – and I am fortunate that I know that even by accident I cannot reach his house. I have seen his house, and I have also seen that he is just an excuse; my real desire is to explore the unknown.

"God was just a name, I had never really thought about all its implications. If you really meet him, what are you going to do? It will be very embarrassing. What are you going to say? And then there is no tomorrow, you have come to a full stop because there is nothing beyond God; God is the very beyond."

I have loved that small poem very much; it gives insight into the human spirit. The human spirit is nothing but a longing – longing for the unknown, longing to know more, longing to be more, longing to explore uncharted seas, unclimbed mountains, unreached stars.

And the joy is not in reaching; the joy is in making the effort, the arduous effort, the dangerous effort. Once you have reached you will have to find a new excuse; otherwise that will be your grave, that will be suicidal.

When Zarathustra says, "I am a wanderer and a mountain climber," he is saying something about you all. He is saying something about the very human spirit.

...I do not like the plains and it seems I cannot sit still for long.
And whatever may yet come to me as fate and experience – a
wandering and a mountain-climbing will be in it...

I will not accept any other destiny because any other destiny will be nothing but death. I will accept the destiny only if wandering and mountain climbing are part of it, if my wandering continues and new mountains and higher mountains and farther away stars are still available to me.

...in the final analysis, one experiences only oneself.

As you go on searching for truth, searching for God, searching for meaning – these are all different names because you cannot go on simply searching for nothing. That needs a totally different insight.

If you understand that wandering in itself is the goal, that there is no goal for which the wandering exists – all goals exist for wandering; wandering itself is the goal – then you need not even have goals. You need not even bother about meaning, about truth, about God; you can go on searching.

But it may be a little difficult. And it will look a little irrational if somebody asks you, "What are you searching for?" If you cannot answer him, and if you simply say, "I am only a pure searcher, it does not matter what." Not to feel embarrassed, you choose any name: you are searching for liberation, you are searching for enlightenment, you are searching for the ultimate truth – beautiful words, and very satisfying to the person who is asking you the question. Neither he is embarrassed nor you are embarrassed.

But in all this wandering, in all this searching, in all this mountain climbing, what do you find? Zarathustra says you find only yourself.

Of course, if you have not wandered, perhaps you may not have found yourself – because all those ecstasies, all those new spaces that you come across help you to discover yourself. Slowly, slowly it dawns upon you that all goals are just excuses.

I am nothing but a longing, a desire for the impossible. This is knowing oneself – the desire for the impossible.

The possible is only for the mediocre minds, for the middle-class people. The impossible is for real giants. They know it cannot be found, that's why it is so important to find it. Knowing perfectly well it has never been found and it is not going to be found gives a great excitement.

The impossible goes on raising human consciousness to higher planes. You may not find anything but you will become a superman.

...in the final analysis one experiences only oneself.
The time has passed when accidents could befall me; and what could still come to me that was not already my own?

Now, no accidents happen to him – what does Zarathustra mean? Accidents happen in your life because you have chosen a certain goal, and if you go astray you miss the goal. You wanted to catch a train and you reached the station late and you missed the train. But if you have no goal except wandering, you cannot go astray. If you are not going to catch a train – no train in particular – you cannot miss the train.

Accidents happen only because we want our lives to be a certain way and something goes wrong, something hinders, something prevents, something comes in the way. You wanted it to be otherwise, and it does not prove to be that way; that is why accidents happen.

Zarathustra says: *The time has passed when accidents could befall me...* Now nothing can be an accident to me because I accept everything. Even the accident is perfectly good, going astray is perfectly good. I was not going toward a particular goal anyway.

This is something of tremendous depth: a man can come to an understanding with life, to such a deep rapport and harmony, that whatever happens is the right thing. He was not asking for something to happen, he was simply available – whatever happens is the right thing, whatever happens, that's what he was wanting to happen.

To go beyond accidents means you have attained a tremendous accord with existence. There is no failure possible, there is no frustration possible. Your silence and your serenity cannot be disturbed.

Gautam Buddha has named this understanding the experience of "suchness." Whatever happens he says, "Such was going to happen." If you were expecting otherwise, then certainly you are sad and you are frustrated – life has not been kind toward you. But to Gautam Buddha, life is always kind, existence is always compassionate because whatever happens, is how it should happen. Gautam Buddha has no other desire than existence itself.

His word is very beautiful. His original word is *tathata*, and because of this word – because he was using it continually... A disciple dies and he says, "It is perfectly okay, his time had come." Nobody dies untimely, although on every grave you will find written, "This poor fellow died untimely." Nobody dies untimely, everybody dies timely, exactly the way that he should die. Because of his use of the word *tathata*, "such is the nature of things," his name became Tathagata – the man who believes in suchness.

You cannot disturb such a man. He will accept the disturbance with an absolute welcome. There is no resistance, there is no reluctance. It is not that he is somehow accepting it, there is total acceptance.

With total acceptance, accidents stop happening and life becomes a totally different experience where there are no frustrations, no accidents, no disasters, where everything is exactly as it should be. You are so centered, so calm and quiet. Nothing stirs in you. Only in this centeredness, in this calmness and quietness, one comes to know oneself.

It is returning, at last it is coming home to me – my own Self and those parts of it that have long been abroad and scattered among all things and accidents.

Now I am gathering to myself all those parts that had fallen apart. At last, I am coming home.

But remember, his home does not mean that he is going to sit still. Wandering is his home, climbing the mountains is his home. He has found his purest longing – it is nothing but a desire to overcome itself. This he calls "returning home" and becoming one: gathering all the scattered parts and creating an organic unity.

And I know one thing more: I stand now before my last summit and before the deed that has been deferred the longest. Alas, I have to climb my most difficult path! Alas, I have started upon my loneliest wandering!

Up to now he was with his disciples. Now he is absolutely alone, and he is on his longest wandering – a wandering that perhaps never ends, that only begins but never ends.

But a man of my sort does not avoid such an hour: the hour that says to him: "Only now do you tread your path of greatness! Summit and abyss – they are now united in one!"

He is saying, "A man of my qualities, who is ready to go on the longest journey knowing perfectly well that perhaps it will never end, and alone, feels deep in the heart that only now is he treading the path of greatness. *Summit and abyss* – the highest and the lowest – both meet in one because now nothing is high to me and nothing is low to me.

"If I fall into the lowest abyss, that will be a wandering; if I reach to the highest summit, that will be a wandering. In my wandering there is no longer any goal." The summit and the abyss have become one: *"...they are now united in one!"*

When such an experience happens you are both, together: your deepest self and your highest self. You are the whole range of all the colors of the rainbow, from one end to the other.

"You are treading your path of greatness: now what was formerly your ultimate danger has become your ultimate refuge!"

What was first thought to be an ultimate danger – to be alone on a journey, which nobody knows whether it ends anywhere or not, whether it leads anywhere or not, that has always been the danger. That's why people remain in crowds. They don't go alone, they remain Christians, they remain Hindus, they remain Mohammedans; they remain Indians, they remain Germans, they remain British.

They are always clinging to some kind of crowd – a nation, a religion, some organization, some political ideology – just to avoid loneliness because somehow we have convinced ourselves that so many millions of people cannot be wrong. But the trouble is, every-body is thinking the same.

In the life of one of the emperors of India, Akbar – he writes in his autobiography, *Akbar Nama*, that a beautiful marble pond was made in his garden especially for swans to be brought from the Himalayas because they are the greatest swans in the world – the whitest and the most beautiful. One of his friends suggested, "Don't fill it with water, fill it with milk as a welcome for those great swans you are bringing from the Himalayas." They very rarely come to the plains; they remain at the highest lake in the world, Mansarovar.

Very few human beings have been able to reach Mansarovar. It is deep in the Himalayas, and at a height that no other lake in the world is. It is the most peaceful lake, and only those swans live there. The idea was good, to welcome them, but where to get so much milk from? The pond was very big.

The friend suggested, "Do one thing: we can inform the whole capital that tomorrow everybody has to bring a bucketful of milk for the king's garden. The swans are coming and it is the duty of the capital to welcome them with milk."

A very wise man who was very intimate with Akbar said to him, "You will be very surprised tomorrow morning."

Akbar said, "Why? What do you mean?"

He said, "Just wait. Tomorrow morning is not far away."

And Akbar was really surprised because the whole pond was full of water! Everybody in the capital had thought that just one bucketful of water in millions of buckets of milk – who will find out who has poured in a bucketful of water? It will be mixed with the milk. But everybody had thought that! Not even a single person had brought milk. Early in the morning – and because they all were bringing water, before sunrise – they all poured their buckets in. And they were very happy that they had managed it. They went back home.

When the king came to look, the wise man was sitting there. He said, "Look at that, your pond full of milk. You don't understand the human mind."

They all think alike – it is a crowd. You are part of a crowd and you think, "So many people cannot be wrong." But they are all are thinking the same, that so many people cannot be wrong. Everybody is thinking the same. Although you may be in a crowd you are alone, and your aloneness remains intact. Why do people want to remain in crowds? What is the fear of being alone?

Zarathustra says, "That has formerly been my greatest danger – to be left alone because then one starts wondering: 'Am I on the right path? Is what I am doing the right thing to do?' And there is nobody else to ask for advice." Left alone, a thousand and one doubts arise, and there is nobody to answer.

People love to live in crowds. There are always people who are ready to give you advice, whether they know anything or not. Giving advice to others is such a joy, and everybody knows that advice is the one thing in the world which is given most, and never taken by anybody. But still people go on giving, free of charge.

But in the crowd one feels cozy. Surrounded by so many people there is every possibility to feel, "Whatever I am doing is right because everybody else is doing it." Alone, great doubts arise, and with them great darkness surrounds you. Alone, where are you going? Is there any God? Does this path lead anywhere, or are you simply going into nowhereness?

But he says: "What was the greatest danger before has become my ultimate refuge. Now I enjoy it; it is my shelter, it is my home. I have dropped all goals, I have made wandering my goal. Now I cannot go wrong."

> *"You are treading your path of greatness: no one shall steal after you here! Your foot itself has extinguished the path behind you, and above that path stands written: Impossibility."*

Unless you accept the challenge of the impossible, your greatness can never blossom to its ultimate peak. Only the impossible brings you to your full flowering; only the impossible brings you your spring, your home.

If you ask me, I will say that God is nothing but another name for the impossible. But it has lost its quality because you have become so acquainted with it – you never think that it is something that is impossible. You have started thinking of God as possible. It has lost its very purpose.

It is better now to change it for Zarathustra's word, *impossibility*. That is his home, that is his refuge, and that is his wandering. And it is bringing his genius, his greatness, his integrity, his individuality to its ultimate grandeur. There is no other achievement except the glory of your own being.

> *"And when all footholds disappear, you must know how to climb upon your own head: how could you climb upward otherwise?"*

One has to transcend oneself. One has to leave oneself behind; one has to go ahead of oneself.

All that you are has to be left behind – your thoughts, your dreams, your imaginations, your prejudices, your philosophies – everything that makes up your personality. You have to leave it the way the snake leaves its old skin, it slips out and never even looks back.

Unless one transcends oneself one cannot experience the impossible. One cannot experience the ultimate in wandering, in searching, one cannot experience the purest longing.

You are just an arrow, and for you there is no target. To understand that you are an arrow – in full speed, going nowhere, you don't have any target – is the most difficult thing to understand about your own being. All other religions seem to be childish – toys for children.

Zarathustra is giving you a challenge which can be accepted only by the very courageous.

"Upon your own head and beyond your own heart!"

Upon your own logic and beyond your own love.

"Now the gentlest part of you must become the hardest....
"In order to see much one must learn to look away from oneself –
every mountain-climber needs this hardness.
"But he who, seeking enlightenment, is over-eager with his eyes,
how could he see more of a thing than its foreground!
"You, however, O Zarathustra, have wanted to behold the ground
of things and their background: so you must climb above yourself –
up and beyond, until you have even your stars under you!"
Yes! To look down upon myself and even upon my stars: that alone
would I call my summit, that has remained for me as my ultimate
summit!...
Man, however, is the most courageous animal: with his courage he
has overcome every animal. With a triumphant shout he has even
overcome every pain; human pain, however, is the deepest pain.
Courage also destroys giddiness at abysses: and where does man
not stand at an abyss?

Wherever you are, however you try to deceive yourself, you are standing at an abyss. All your consolations are false. All your defenses are just imaginary. Are you not standing at an abyss each moment of your life? – because the next moment can be your death, and that is the greatest abyss.

Is seeing itself not – seeing abysses?

The more you are a seer, the more you see the abysses around you. The blind man can stand happily by the side of an abyss not knowing there is an abyss. Just one wrong step and he will be lost forever, but only a blind man can stand there without any fear. All seeing is seeing of the abysses. But also, if you want to see the summits of your being you will have to see the abysses.

If you don't have a goal, if you don't want to reach anywhere, if the very exploring is a joy unto itself, if discovering new spaces out-side and inside is a bliss and a benediction to you, then abysses and summits don't make any difference. They become one – they are one. And man has that much courage, one just has to awaken it; it is fast asleep.

Once your courage is awake, once your courage roars like a lion, you feel for the first time the thrill of life, the joy of life, the dance of life.

> *Courage is the best destroyer: courage also destroys pity. Pity,*
> *however, is the deepest abyss: as deeply as man looks into life, so*
> *deeply does he look also into suffering.*
> *Courage, however, is the best destroyer, courage that attacks: it*
> *destroys even death, for it says: "Was that life? Well then! Once*
> *more!"*

I am reminded of a small anecdote. In the Soviet Union, in the middle of the night, a KGB man knocks on a door and shouts, "Is Ginsberg inside?"

Somebody opens the door, and the KGB man says, "I am from the KGB. Is Ginsberg inside?"

The man said, "Ginsberg? He is dead."

The KGB man said, "Dead? Who are you? What is your name?"

The man said, "My name? My name is Ginsberg."

The KGB man said, "Are you insane or something? Just now you said that Ginsberg is dead."

The man laughed and he said, "Do you call this living? Even in the middle of the night one cannot sleep peacefully – do you call this living?"

If, at the time of death, death inquires of you, "Would you like to live your life, the same life that you have lived, one time more?" What do you think your answer is going to be? I don't think that any intelligent man would be ready to live this whole tragedy again – exactly the same wife, the same husband; exactly the same drama, the same dialogues.

But a man who has lived life not as a misery, but as an explo-ration into new experiences: always moving, always going upward, always searching for something better, always creating himself, always destroying all that is rubbish in him and bringing out the best; perhaps he may say, "Well then, once more – no harm!"

But only a man who has really lived intensively and totally and who has not been lukewarm and tepid, who has burned his life's torch at both ends together, will be ready to go through life again because he knows he can change everything that has been. He can find new spaces, he can find new mountains to climb, he can find new stars to reach, he can trust in himself. He knows his courage and he knows that to live dangerously is the only way to live.

But there is a great triumphant shout in such a saying. He who has ears to hear, let him hear.

Live in such a way that if life is given to you again it will not be a repetition. But it is already a repetition. You don't need another life; even this life is just a repetition.

I have heard about a man who married eight times. Obviously the story must be from California because you cannot find greater idiots anywhere else. Otherwise, one wife is enough for any intelligent man. For those who are really intelligent, even one is not needed. But eight wives... And when he married the eighth time, after two months he realized that he had married this woman once before, but it was a long time ago.

Another thing he found: each time he had tried to find a new woman, but within six months the story would become the same. It is a strange thing – he goes to faraway lands to find a new woman, but every woman turns out, within six months, to be the same. But he never understood that *he* is the same, his liking is the same, his choice is the same. So whenever he finds a new woman, it is always the same woman he likes. He has not changed, he is only changing the woman.

But who is going to choose? The same man, who had chosen the first woman, will choose the second for the same reasons. Only a certain face appeals to him, a certain hairdo, a certain way of walking; just all kinds of stupid things which don't make any essential difference. Again he will fall into the same trap, and eight times... It is now happening in many people's lives because in California the average time for marriage stability is three years. It is the same average for any man to remain in one job, the same average for any man to remain in one town.

Strange – three years, and the man gets bored with the job, with the wife, with the town, with the friends. He changes everything, but he will again find, within three months, that he has again entered a similar type of story. And within three years the conclusion is always the same tragedy.

In the East, all three great religions – Hinduism, Buddhism and Jainism – have used the idea of reincarnation; that you don't have only one life like in Christianity and Judaism and Mohammedanism. Those three religions born outside of India have only one life. They have not understood the great psychological insight of the East: the East accepts that you will have many, many lives. You had many before, and you will have many in the future.

The idea was to create in you a sense of utter boredom. Just think, you have lived many times, you have done the same stupid things many times, you are still doing them, and you are bound to do them in the future also. Many, many times, thousands of lives, and you will be just sitting in a grocery store, tending the shop, fighting with your wife, complaining to everybody about your misfortunes. The film is the same, the story is the same, the dialogues are the same, the actors are the same.

The idea was used by these three religions to give you a clear-cut sense of utter boredom. If you want to change, change! Otherwise you will be moving like a wheel, and the same spokes will go on coming on top and down, on top and down, and the same misery…

If you want to change then don't postpone it for tomorrow, from this very moment start exploring. And remember not to be repetitive. Always look for something new, something fresh – because there is really no goal except the journey. So make the most of it. Make it as beautiful as possible, as enchanting, as creative as you have the capacity to make it. And you have infinite capacity, it is just dormant.

Zarathustra wants to provoke you to be a seeker of the impossible, to be a mountain climber, to be a wanderer on the paths where nobody has ever wandered and perhaps nobody will ever wander.

Only this newness, this youth, can be called authentic living; otherwise, you are simply vegetating. What kind of vegetable you are does not matter, cabbage or cauliflower, because I have heard that the only difference between cabbages and cauliflowers is that cauliflowers have university degrees and cabbages are uneducated!

To be a man needs guts because to be a man means a continuous overcoming, a transcendence every day. Where the sunset leaves you, the sunrise should not find you there, and where the sunrise leaves you, the sunset should not find you there.

Be a wanderer of the soul. Be a wanderer in the innermost depths of consciousness.

This is the only true religion, which only a very few people, like Zarathustra, have introduced to humanity. But they have been either totally ignored or they have been misunderstood.

It will be fortunate if you can understand this man Zarathustra because he can give you the incentive to go on a long journey, which will end in finding yourself.

...Thus spake Zarathustra.

rising to the heights

Of the Three Evil Things

...I will now place the three most evil things upon the scales and weigh them well and humanly....

Sensual pleasure, lust for power, selfishness: *these three have hitherto been cursed the most and held in the worst and most unjust repute – these three will I weigh well and humanly....*

Sensual pleasure: a sweet poison only to the withered, but to the lion-willed the great restorative and reverently-preserved wine of wines.

Sensual pleasure: the great symbolic happiness of a higher happiness and highest hope....

...to many that are stranger to one another than man and woman: and who has fully conceived how strange *man and woman are to one another!...*

Lust for power: the scourge of fire of the hardest-hearted; the cruel torment reserved by the cruelest for himself; the dark flame of living bonfires....

Lust for power: before its glance man crawls and bends and toils and becomes lower than the swine or the snake – until at last the cry of the great contempt burst from him....

Lust for power: which, however, rises enticingly even to the pure and the solitary and up to self-sufficient heights, glowing like a love that paints purple delights enticingly on earthly heavens.

Lust for power: but who shall call it lust, *when the height longs to stoop down after power! Truly, there is no sickness and lust in such a longing and descent!*

That the lonely height may not always be solitary and sufficient to itself; that the mountain may descend to the valley and the wind of the heights to the lowlands –

Oh who shall find the rightful baptismal and virtuous name for such a longing! "Bestowing virtue" – that is the name Zarathustra once gave the unnamable.

And then it also happened – and truly, it happened for the first time! – that his teaching glorified selfishness, *the sound, healthy selfishness that issues from a mighty soul –*

from a mighty soul, to which pertains the exalted body, the beautiful, victorious, refreshing body, around which everything becomes a mirror....

It banishes from itself all that is cowardly; it says: Bad – that is to say, cowardly!...

Timid mistrustfulness seems base to it, as do all who desire oaths....

Entirely hateful and loathsome to it is he who will never defend himself, who swallows down poisonous spittle and evil looks, the too-patient man who puts up with everything, is content with everything: for that is the nature of slaves.

Whether one be servile before gods and divine kicks, or before men and the silly opinions of men: it spits at slaves of all kinds, this glorious selfishness!...

...to ill-use selfishness – precisely that *has been virtue and called virtue. And "selfless" – that is what, with good reason, all these world-weary cowards...wished to be!*

But now the day, the transformation, the sword of judgment, the great noontide *comes to them all: then many things shall be revealed!*

And he who declares the Ego healthy and holy and selfishness glorious – truly, he, a prophet, declares too what he knows: "Behold, it comes, it is near, the great noontide!"

...Thus spake Zarathustra.

All the teachers before Zarathustra, and even after him, have looked at things with a very prejudiced mind. They have not allowed the multidimensionality of every experience. They have imposed a certain dimension and conditioned human mind to look at things only in a certain way. Zarathustra's great contribution is that he helps man to look at things in new ways – absolutely new, fresh, and immensely enlightening. You may be shocked sometimes because he will be speaking against your prejudices. You have to be courageous enough to put aside all your prejudices.

To understand this man of great insight, who looks at things not according to a certain preconceived ideology, but looks at things as they are, in themselves... He does not impose any meaning; on the contrary, he tries to find whether there is any meaning in things themselves. He is very objective, very realistic and absolutely sane. He is not obsessed with any idea and he does not want to propound a certain philosophy or a certain religion.

His approach is so totally different. He teaches you how to see clearly. He does not teach you what to see, he simply teaches you how to see clearly.

The clarity of your vision will bring you the truth. He is not going to hand over the truth to you like something ready-made. He does not want truth to be so cheap. And anything which is very cheap cannot be true. Truth demands you be a gambler so that you can risk everything at the stake. Truth cannot be a possession of yours. On the contrary, if you are ready to be possessed by truth, then only can you have it.

What he is going to say this evening is so contrary to all the religions, all the so-called moralities, that unless you can put your mind out of the way, you will not be able to hear him and you will not be able to understand. He is throwing diamonds on your path. But you can remain blind; you can keep your eyes closed just so that you are not disturbed in your preconceived beliefs.

He is bent upon disturbing you because unless you are disturbed you cannot move, you cannot progress, you cannot have any excitement to reach to farther away stars, you cannot be stirred by the longing to become a superman. You have to be shaken, and shaken mercilessly. Only later on will you understand: that was compassion, true compassion.

To support you in your convenient lies is not love. It makes you feel good, but it is very destructive – it is evil. It destroys your possibilities of growth. And Zarathustra has only one single-pointed teaching: man should transcend himself. But why should he transcend if he is very comfortable? His comfort has to be destroyed. His conveniences have to be taken away. His prejudices have to be shattered. His religions, his gods, his philosophies all have to be burned. He has to be left utterly nude, just like a newly born baby.

Only from there, from that innocence, from that newness, from that point the superman, the only hope for humanity, can arise and replace this rotten, disgusting mankind. Because we are living in it we have become accustomed to its rottenness. We have become accustomed to his disgusting smell.

Kahlil Gibran has a small story...

A woman has come from the village to the city to sell fish. She is a fisherman's wife. In the city, after selling her fish, she comes across an old friend. They used to study in the school together, but the woman was very rich and they had not seen each other for years. So the rich woman invited her, at least for the night, to stay with her. She had a beautiful palace, she had a beautiful garden, and she was certain that her friend would be immensely pleased.

Before going to bed she brought many, many roses and put them by the side of the bed of her guest. But time went on passing and the poor woman could not sleep. She turned over again and again, and because she could not sleep her host also could not sleep. Finally the host asked, "What is the matter?"

The fisherman's wife said, "You will have to forgive me. Just give me the clothes in which I had brought the fish to sell. Sprinkle them with a little water and remove these roses and bring those clothes back to me. If I can smell fish I will fall asleep immediately. These roses will not allow me to sleep."

The roses are removed, the rotten clothes, dirty, are sprinkled with water and the whole room starts smelling fishy. The woman is immensely happy and she says, "Now I can sleep perfectly well. I'm accustomed to this perfume. Roses don't suit me."

We are accustomed to this humanity – that's why we don't see its disgustingness. We don't see its ugliness. We don't see its jealousy. We don't see its lovelessness. We don't see its unintelligent, stupid, mediocre behavior. Listening to Zarathustra you can become aware of a totally different way of seeing mankind.

Zarathustra says:

...I will now place the three most evil things upon the scales and weigh them well and humanly.

I would like you to remember the word *humanly* because all the so-called religions and spiritual philosophies have been valuing things very inhumanly. Hence, I want you to remember the word *humanly*.

Zarathustra is immensely in love with man. He is no enemy; he is a friend. He hates the present state because he knows you can go far away, you can reach high peaks. This state is not what you are meant for. His hate toward the present mankind is because of his deep love for your future, for the distant goal of the superman. He is absolutely against inhuman values. All the religions expect you to follow inhuman values.

If you look into the religious scriptures of all the religions you will be surprised: what they are asking you to do is so unnatural that you cannot fulfill it. Certainly their purpose of asking is something that you are not aware of. They also know you cannot fulfill the demands that they are making on you. But then why are they making those demands? Their hidden purpose is to make you feel guilty. And the only way to make you feel guilty is to ask something unnatural, which you cannot do, whatever way you try. You are going to fail.

I have heard...

A man was purchasing a few toys for his children in a toyshop. The salesman brought something out, and he said, "This is the very latest device in the world of toys. It is a jigsaw puzzle." The man was a professor of mathematics, so he became immediately interested in it. He tried it this way and that way. He tried it in many ways and the ultimate result was always failure. He said to the salesman, "I am a professor of mathematics and I cannot figure it out. How do you expect small children to succeed in solving the puzzle?"

The salesman laughed. He said, "It is not made to be solved. It represents man's actual situation. Whatever you do, it doesn't matter what, the puzzle cannot be solved. It is a very modern, a very contemporary understanding of humanity."

All the religions have been giving you puzzles that are basically and intrinsically insoluble. And their purpose is to make you feel guilty, a failure, frustrated, miserable, unsuccessful, unworthy, undeserving. They want to destroy your pride, your dignity because the more your pride and your dignity is destroyed, the more you will be just like the camel – kneeling down and ready to be loaded. You will understand that it is your fate to be a camel; you are not a lion and there is no point in pretending to be a lion.

You are born to be a slave – that's the whole strategy of all the religions, all the political ideologies. They have a single intention: to make every human being feel that he is born to be a slave, to be a worshipper of a fictitious God, to kneel down and to pray.

The moment you accept yourself to be guilty, undeserving, unworthy, you lose self-respect; you lose love for yourself. And if you cannot love yourself, how can you expect anybody else to love you? It is almost always a shock when somebody says to you, "I love you." You cannot believe it. Nobody believes it, for the simple reason: "I cannot love myself and this poor fellow is saying he loves me. That means only one thing: he does not know me! Once he knows me all love will disappear."

Lovers are great if they cannot meet, if the society or the parents or the religion or something comes in their way and does not allow them to meet. All great love stories are about lovers who could not meet. I have been wondering… It is strange: there is not a single great love story about lovers who marry. Every old story ends when the lovers marry. It says, "After that they lived in happiness forever." But it does not give any details. The story ends there.

I know perfectly well that if Laila and Majnu or Shiri and Farhad or Sohini and Mahival – the three great lovers of the East – by chance had got married, they would have been standing in a court of divorce. There would have never been any great story about them.

The whole work of centuries is only one: to make you hate yourself; not to allow you to accept yourself. Of course they don't say it so clearly. Their ways are devious, but Zarathustra is very clear what their ways are, and how they have destroyed human beings and the possibilities of this beautiful planet being turned into a living paradise – not a dream, but a reality.

Sensual pleasure, lust for power, selfishness: *these three have*

hitherto been cursed the most and held in the worst and most
unjust repute – these three will I weigh well and humanly.

That he never forgets: don't try to impose upon yourself inhuman standards which are only going to cripple you, which are only going to cut your wings, which are only going to enslave you in such a deep psychological slavery that it will be very difficult to get out of – because one tends to cling to it. It seems to be safer, it seems to be more convenient, it seems to be more acceptable to the society.

The more a man tries to be disciplining himself into inhuman values, of course he is going to be just a hypocrite. But the crowds will respect him as a saint, for the simple reason that they cannot do it. They have tried, but this man must be great; he *is* doing it. Most probably he has a dual personality. He has two faces: one to show to the world and one which is a private thing, which he lives in secrecy. Life goes underground. On the surface he pretends all those values which are humanly impossible.

The first is sensual pleasure – condemned by every religion without any conditions. But if you look humanly at sensual pleasure… a few things to be remembered. One is: if you renounce sensual pleasure, which is what all your so-called saints and priests are asking you to do, you will become more and more insensitive. It is sensual pleasure which keeps your senses alive, thrilled, dancing. It is sensual pleasure which keeps your sensitivity at its maximum. If you renounce sensual pleasure you are renouncing your sensitivity. You will see a roseflower, but you will not see the beauty of it. You will see the full moon in the night, but you will not see the beauty of it because to see the beauty, you need sensitivity.

If you cannot see the beauty of a woman, how can you see the beauty of a starry night? How can you see the beauty of flowers? If you are not sensitive you cannot experience the joys of music, the ecstatic pleasure of paintings, sculptures, poetry.

All that is great, all that is contributed by the great geniuses to humanity, you become utterly blind to, deaf to. Your sensitivity slowly, slowly becomes dead. And if all your senses become dead you are just a corpse. What is the difference between a corpse and a living man?

The living man is sensitive. All his senses are functioning at the optimum. He can hear the subtlest notes of music and he can see the profoundest beauty of art; he can feel the joy of great poetry. But this is possible only if he allows his sensual pleasure – uninhibited, without any conditionings.

Zarathustra says the first is:

Sensual pleasure: a sweet poison only to the withered, but to the lion-willed the great restorative and reverently-preserved wine of wines.

Zarathustra is certainly unparalleled. When it comes to stating the truth, he simply states it without ever bothering whether anybody is going to listen to him or not. It may go against the whole world, but he will stand alone, will remain with the truth.

He is saying, sensual pleasure is: ...*a sweet poison only to the withered...* Only to the weak. And the weak have been ruling over the strong. The unintelligent are deciding life patterns for the intelligent. The crowd is making religions to live by, commandments to be followed. All these moralities, ethical codes, are created by the withered and the weak, the retarded and the stupid.

They are perfectly good for them, but they forget completely that everybody is not a sheep; there are lions also. And the lion cannot be forced to be a sheep. You can encage the lion, you can imprison the lion. And that's what all strong-willed people in the world feel: they are imprisoned – imprisoned by the small, imprisoned by the weak, imprisoned by the crowd. Certainly the sheep are in the majority.

And just because of their numbers they have been deciding lifestyles which may be suitable to them, but which are only imprisonment and death to those who are strong enough. There should be a clear-cut distinction: something can be poison to someone, and the same thing can be a medicine to someone else. It all depends on to whom it is being given.

...*a sweet poison only to the withered, but to the lion-willed the great restorative and reverently-preserved wine of wines.* Zarathustra is saying something of immense importance and greatness: reverently-preserved. He is making sensual pleasure something sacred. If it destroys you it is not the sensual pleasure, it is your weakness. Be strong! But your so-called religious leaders have been telling you just the opposite: renounce sensual pleasures and remain weak. And the more you renounce them, the weaker you will become because you will lose all restorative power, all rejuvenating power. You will lose the contact with existence because it is through the senses that you are connected with existence. If you close your senses you have already prepared your grave.

Zarathustra will say just the opposite. If sensual pleasure destroys you that means you need to be stronger. And discipline should be given to you so that you can become stronger. Sensual pleasure has not to be renounced; weakness has to be renounced. And everybody should be made so strong that he can enjoy the *wine of wines* without being destroyed by it, but on the contrary, made stronger, younger, fresher.

Sensuality has been so condemned that it has made the whole world of human beings utterly weak, insensitive, unconnected with life. Most of your roots have been cut; only a few roots have been left so that you can just survive in the name of life.

Sensual pleasure: the great symbolic happiness of a higher happiness and highest hope.

Sensual pleasure has to be understood as an indication that even greater happiness is possible. It all depends on your being artful. It all depends how you use your life energies. It all depends if you don't stop at sensual pleasure. Sensual pleasure is only an arrow indicating that there are greater pleasures, that there are greater happinesses, that there are greater fulfillments.

But if you renounce sensual pleasure... It is as if you see on a milestone an arrow showing you that this is not the place to stop, go on! The renouncers are saying, "Erase that arrow. Renounce that milestone." But then who is going to indicate to you that you have still a long way to go?

Until you reach the greatest joy of life – sensuous pleasure is only the beginning, not the end. But if you deny the beginning you have denied the end. It is such a simple logic, but sometimes whatever is obvious is easily forgotten. All the religions have been teaching you, "If you deny sensuous pleasure, only then will you be able to have spiritual blissfulness." It is absurd and illogical.

Sensuous pleasure is going to be a stepping-stone toward spiritual blissfulness. You are destroying the very stepping-stone. You will never reach the higher stage – you have removed the ladder. The ladder is something to be transcended, but not renounced! Remember the difference between transcendence and renunciation.

Zarathustra will say, "Transcend but never renounce because if you renounce there is nothing to transcend." Enjoy the sensuous pleasures in all their variety and as intensely as possible. Exhaust them, so that suddenly you become aware: "The world of sensuous pleasures is finished and I have to go beyond." But the sensuous pleasure has shown you the way. You will be grateful to it; you will not be against it. It has not taken anything away from you; it has only given to you.

Sensual pleasure: the great symbolic happiness of a higher happiness and highest hope....
...to many that are stranger to one another than man and woman...

The sensuous pleasure is a bridge between man and woman. And certainly they are strangers to one another.

This is not something unfortunate. The greater the distance is between man and woman, the greater is the attraction. The more different they are, the more there is a pull to come together. The more they are strangers to each other, the more there is a deep inquiry to understand each other.

If I have been against all kinds of sexual perversions, if I have been against homosexuality in particular, my basic reason is spiritual – because a man loving another man or a woman loving another woman don't have any magnetic pull; they don't have any tension. They are so alike, they are almost the same. There is not going to be any inquiry; there is not going to be any exploration. They are not going to understand anything more than they know already because they know themselves – what can the other man be, more than they are?

Homosexuality is absolutely unspiritual because it cannot give a sharpness to your sensuality. And it cannot make your sensual pleasure an indicator of higher happiness. Homosexuality is a kind of being stuck. It is no longer a journey. You are not going anywhere.

The meeting of men and women is a journey; it is an exploration. It is an effort to understand the polar opposite, it is to understand the dialectics of life. It is a great lesson. And without this lesson you cannot move higher in consciousness, in happiness, in spirituality.

But man has fallen so low. Zarathustra was very predictive – that the days are coming soon when man will become so small that he will not be worthy even to be called man. It seems those days have come.

One of the reasons for Holland's parliament deciding that I cannot enter Holland was that I have been speaking against homosexuality. Even I could not believe it: Holland's religion is homosexuality? But it certainly shows that the members of the parliament in Holland and the prime minister and the cabinet of Holland all seem to be homosexual because not a single person stood up and said, "This is derogatory to the whole nation. What do you mean by it – if a person has spoken against homosexuality, has he committed a crime? Are you a nation of homosexuals? Is he against your nationality?"

When I heard this I immediately informed my people, "Tell the parliament that the name of Holland should be changed: it should be 'homosexual land' – that will be more appropriate." But man has fallen very low. And the reason he has fallen so low is because your saints have been teaching you to be celibates, which is against nature. It is celibacy which is the cause of homosexuality.

And now one American bishop has come out and openly declared – and he has not been refuted by the Pope or by any other Christian association or Christian church – he has openly said that celibacy does not include homosexuality. You can be celibate and you can be homosexual. Celibacy simply means you cannot be heterosexual. It only prevents men meeting women; it does not prevent men making love to another man or a woman making love to another woman. It is not against lesbianism or against homosexuality.

And the Pope is silent! His silence says much because he knows perfectly well that more than fifty percent of his bishops, archbishops, cardinals, priests are all homosexuals.

Homosexuality was born in monasteries – Christian, Buddhist, Jaina. Wherever so many celibates were forced to live together, a single sex... Nature finds some way, however perverted it may be. These people who have been against sensual pleasure have destroyed man in such a subtle way and have created a perverted humanity. And they are still our leaders. They are still our guides to spirituality.

...and who has fully conceived how strange *man and woman are to one another!*

Only a man of deep sensual experience can understand the vast difference and the uniqueness of men and women. There is no question of equality and there is no question of inequality; they are simply unique beings. And between them only friendship is possible.

This whole nonsense of marriage makes the man important. The woman becomes just a shadow. Why, after marriage, does a woman have to take her husband's name? These are subtle ways to make it clear to her that now she is secondary. She no longer has her own identity; her husband is her identity. Naturally, marriage can never be peaceful. Wherever there is an effort of domination there is going to be conflict and struggle. And all marriages create only hell.

> *Lust for power: the scourge of fire of the hardest-hearted; the cruel torment reserved by the cruelest for himself; the dark flame of living bonfires....*
> *Lust for power, before its glance man crawls and bends and toils and becomes lower than the swine or the snake – until at last the cry of the great contempt bursts from him....*
> *Lust for power: which, however, rises enticingly even to the pure and the solitary and up to self-sufficient heights, glowing like a love that paints purple delights enticingly on earthly heavens.*
> *Lust for power: but who shall call it lust, when the height longs to stoop down after power! Truly, there is no sickness and lust in such a longing and descent!*

One has to look at the whole thing. Lust for power has created slavery, has destroyed humanity in many ways. Lust for power is burning in every heart. Zarathustra is not in favor of this kind of lust for power – it is destructive and ugly.

But there can be a creative way, and that creative thing he calls will to power, not lust for power. Will to power is a totally different phenomenon, but the religions have not made the distinction. For them, lust for power is all – there is nothing in it which can have something to contribute. But Zarathustra feels there is so much potential in it that it can become the greatest creative force in the world. But it has not to be lust. And it cannot even be called lust.

Lust for power: but who shall call it lust, *when the height longs to stoop down after power!* Truly, there is no sickness and lust in such a longing and descent! Will to power makes a great change. Will to power simply means no power over others. Lust for power means power over others. Will to power means becoming in oneself more and more powerful, more and more radiant, more and more strong, more and more integrated, more and more a lion, an individual.

Will to power has nothing to do with the other. It is your own exercise of rising to the heights. It is your own discipline to reach to the highest peak of your being. It is not destructive of anybody; on the contrary, it can be an inspiration for others. It has to be an inspiration for others. It can be a great incentive: if a single man who was one day amongst you is now on the highest peak of consciousness, it may create an urge, a longing, a will – which is asleep in you, which is dormant in you – that you can also be a high peak, that it is also within your capacity.

Will to power is simply will to be oneself – will to freedom, will to create, will to attain immortality, will to proclaim to the world, "I have always been here and I will be always here." It is will to eternity.

But the religions have taken only the negative side: they have never talked about the positive side. And with the negative side they have condemned the positive side also. They deceived humanity; they never made any distinction that everything has its positivity, its negativity. They condemned the negative and that was right, but they never praised the positive, and that is where there cunningness is.

> That the lonely height may not always be solitary and sufficient to itself; that the mountain may descend to the valley and the wind of the heights to the lowlands –
> Oh who shall find the rightful baptismal and virtuous name for such a longing! "Bestowing virtue" – that is the name Zarathustra once gave the unnamable.
> And then it also happened – and truly, it happened for the first time! – that his teaching glorified selfishness...

About selfishness, certainly he is absolutely the first man in the whole of history who glorified selfishness:

> ...the sound, healthy selfishness that issues from a mighty soul – from a mighty soul, to which pertains the exalted body, the beautiful, victorious, refreshing body, around which everything becomes a mirror....

It banishes from itself all that is cowardly; it says: Bad – that is to say, cowardly!

According to Zarathustra the only thing bad is cowardliness and the only thing good is courageousness. Out of courage are born all the virtues, and out of cowardliness are born all the sins, all the crimes.

Timid mistrustfulness seems base to it, as do all who desire oaths....
Entirely hateful and loathsome to it is he who will never defend
himself, who swallows down poisonous spittle and evil looks, the
too-patient man who puts up with everything, is content with
everything: for that is the nature of slaves.
Whether one be servile before gods and divine kicks, or before men
and the silly opinions of men: it spits at slaves of all kinds, this
glorious selfishness!...
...to ill-use selfishness – precisely that has been virtue and called
virtue. And "selfless" – that is what, with good reasons, all these
world-weary cowards...wished to be!

Zarathustra is saying that selfishness is simply the nature of things. But the cowards want unselfishness to be the virtue because in unselfishness, the cowards are going to be the winners.

In India you will find beggars all over the country. And every beggar is saying, "Give me something. Giving to the beggars is virtue, and you will be rewarded immensely for it." Now the very existence of beggars should show that the society is sick, that the society is insane; that it goes on producing children, which it cannot feed. That it is absolutely illogical that one section of society will accumulate all the money of the land and millions will be left starving.

You will be surprised to know that half of the wealth of the whole of India is in Mumbai – one city. A country of nine hundred million people is utterly poor, undernourished; even to manage to get one meal a day is to be very fortunate. There are millions of people who are simply living on the roots of the trees. They eat the roots of the trees; fruits they cannot afford. And by the end of the century near-about half a billion people will die of starvation just in this country. I am not talking about the whole world – because this is going to happen almost all over the world.

Virtue should be intelligence, virtue should be logic, virtue should be reasonability. But giving to the beggars maintains the beggars. Those beggars produce more beggars. Those beggars get married. Those beggars produce children because it is economically profitable to have children because those children start begging. The more children you have, the better is your profession.

Zarathustra is saying, "Selfishness is the only virtue; unselfishness has been the desire of the cowardly – that they should be helped, that somebody should protect them, that somebody should provide food for them, that somebody should take care of their sicknesses, that somebody else is responsible if they are sick, if they are hungry, if they are starving. Nobody is responsible for that."

A society which is sane will prevent all kinds of people who need unselfish service.

We can manage a society which is healthy; we can manage a society which is rich, comfortably rich, comfortably healthy. But this is possible only if everybody takes his responsibility on his own shoulders.

That's what he means by selfishness. And if you have too much to share, that should be your joy, not a duty. That should be your joy, not a virtue.

> But now the day, the transformation, the sword of judgment, the great noontide *comes to them all: then many things shall be revealed!*
> And he who declares the Ego healthy and holy and selfishness glorious – truly, he, a prophet, declares too what he knows: "Behold, it comes, it is near, the great noontide!"

Zarathustra calls the greatest moment in humanity's life: ...*the great noontide* – when selfishness will be simply healthy, when everything that has been condemned before will be dropped and everything that is natural and human will be declared as our religion, as our spirituality. Nature itself is our religion, and there is no need for any other religion.

"Behold it comes, it is near, the great noontide!"

...*Thus spake Zarathustra.*

seriousness is a sin

Of Laughter and Dance

What has been the greatest sin here on earth? Was it not the saying of him who said: "Woe to those who laugh!"

Did he himself find on earth no reason for laughter? If so, he sought badly. Even a child could find reasons.

He – did not love sufficiently: otherwise he would also have loved us, the laughers! But he hated and jeered at us, he promised us wailing and gnashing of teeth.

Does one then straightway have to curse where one does not love? That – seems to me bad taste. But that is what he did, this uncompromising man. He sprang from the mob.

And he himself did not love sufficiently: otherwise he would not have been so angry that he was not loved. Great love does not desire love – it desires more.

Avoid all such uncompromising men! They are a poor, sick type, a mob type: they look upon this life with an ill will, they have an evil eye for this earth.

Avoid all such uncompromising men! They have heavy feet and sultry hearts – they do not know how to dance. How could the earth be light to such men!...

This laugher's crown, this rose-wreath crown: I myself have set this crown on my head, I myself have canonized my laughter. I have found no other strong enough for it today.
Zarathustra the dancer, Zarathustra the light, who beckons with his wings, ready for flight, beckoning to all birds, prepared and ready, blissfully light-hearted:
Zarathustra the prophet, Zarathustra the laughing prophet, no impatient nor uncompromising man, one who loves jumping and escapades; I myself have set this crown on my head!...
You higher men, the worst about you is: none of you has learned to dance as a man ought to dance – to dance beyond yourselves!
What does it matter that you are failures!
How much is still possible! So learn to laugh beyond yourselves!
Lift up your hearts, you fine dancers, high! higher! and do not forget to laugh well!
This laugher's crown, this rose-wreath crown: to you, my brothers, do I throw this crown! I have canonized laughter; you Higher Men, learn – to laugh!...
"This is my morning, my day begins: rise up now, rise up, great noontide!"
Thus spake Zarathustra and left his cave, glowing and strong, like a morning sun emerging from behind dark mountains.

Zarathustra is absolutely right when he says:

What has been the greatest sin here on earth? Was it not the saying of him who said: "Woe to those who laugh!"

But all your so-called saints are saying that, all your religions are saying that, all your so-called great men are saying that. And they are not saying it without any reason.

One of the cruelest things done to man is to make him sad and serious. This has to be done because without making man sad and serious, it is impossible to make him a slave – a slave in all the dimensions of slavery: spiritually a slave to some fictitious God, to some fictitious heaven and hell; psychologically a slave because sadness, seriousness are not natural, they have to be forced upon

the mind and the mind falls into fragments, is shattered; and phys-
ically a slave also because a man who cannot laugh, cannot be
really healthy and whole.

Laughter is not one-dimensional; it has all the three dimensions
of man's being. When you laugh your body joins it, your mind joins
it, your being joins it. In laughter the distinctions disappear, the divisions disappear, the schizophrenic personality disappears. But it was
against those who wanted to exploit man: the kings, the priests, the
cunning politicians. Their whole effort was somehow to make man
weaker, sick – make man miserable and he will never revolt.

Taking man's laughter away from him is taking his very life
away. Taking laughter away from man is spiritual castration. Have
you seen the difference between bulls and bullocks? They were born
the same, but the bullocks have been castrated. And unless they are
castrated, you cannot use them as slaves to carry your burden, to
draw your carts. You cannot put bulls ahead of your cart – the bull is
so powerful, it is impossible to keep him in control; he has an individuality of his own. But the bullock is a very faraway echo of his
real being, just a shadow. You have destroyed him.

To create slaves, man has been destroyed in the same way.
Laughter has been condemned continually as childish, as insane; at
the most you are allowed to smile. The difference between a smile
and laughter is the same as between the bullock and the bull.
Laughter is total. The smile is just an exercise of the lips; the smile is
just a mannerism. Laughter knows no mannerism, no etiquette – it
is wild, and its wildness has all the beauty.

But the vested interests, whether of money or of organized religions or of the rulers, were all agreed on one thing: man has to be
weakened, made miserable, made afraid – has to be forced to live in
a kind of paranoia. Only then will he kneel down on his knees before
wooden or stone statues. Only then will he be ready to serve anybody who is powerful.

Laughter brings your energy back to you. Every fiber of your
being becomes alive, and every cell of your being starts dancing.
Zarathustra is right when he says that the greatest sin against
man done on the earth is that he has been prohibited from
laughing. The implications are deep because when you are prohibited from laughing certainly you are prohibited from being joyous,
you are prohibited from singing a song of celebration, you are

prohibited from dancing just out of sheer blissfulness.

By prohibiting laughter, all that is beautiful in life, all that makes life livable and lovable, all that gives meaning to life is destroyed. It is the ugliest strategy used against man.

Seriousness is a sin. And remember, seriousness does not mean sincerity – sincerity is altogether a different phenomenon. A serious man cannot laugh, cannot dance, cannot play. He is always controlling himself; he has been brought up in such a way that he has become a jailer to himself. The sincere man can laugh sincerely, can dance sincerely, can rejoice sincerely. Sincerity has nothing to do with seriousness.

Seriousness is simply sickness of the soul, and only sick souls can be converted into slaves. And all the vested interests need a humanity which is not rebellious, which is very willing, almost begging, to be slaves.

Did he himself find on earth no reason for laughter? If so, he sought badly. Even a child could find reasons.

In fact, only children are found to be giggling and laughing; and the grown-ups think that children can be forgiven because they are ignorant – they are as yet uncivilized, as yet primitive. The whole effort of parents, of society, of teachers, of priests is how to civilize them, how to make them serious, how to make them behave like slaves, not like independent individuals.

You are not supposed to have your own opinions. You just have to be a Christian or a Hindu or a Mohammedan; you have to be a communist or a fascist or a socialist. You are not supposed to have your own opinions; you are not supposed to be yourself. You are allowed to be part of a crowd – and to be part of a crowd is nothing but becoming a cog in a wheel. You have committed suicide.

Zarathustra is asking, "Can't you find anything on the earth that makes you laugh, that makes you dance, that makes you rejoice? Even children can find reasons." But your mind has been filled with so many prejudices that your eyes are almost blind, your heart is almost dead; you have been turned into living corpses.

He – did not love sufficiently: otherwise he would also have loved us, the laughers!

In fact, in society the man who laughs totally – a belly laugh – is not respected. You have to look serious; that shows that you are civilized and sane. Laughing is for children and for the insane, or for the primitive.

I cannot conceive that Jesus ever laughed in his life. Of course, he cannot laugh on the cross; for that, a far greater man is needed – perhaps a Zarathustra – because there have been people who have laughed on the cross. Just go into any church and see Jesus on the cross. Naturally he is serious, and his seriousness fills the whole church; to laugh there seems to be out of place. There is no mention anywhere that Jesus ever laughed in his life; it is obvious that the only begotten son of God has to be very serious. Nobody has ever heard that God has laughed either.

Jesus cannot laugh because he is full of expectations; and those expectations are going to turn into frustrations. Even on the cross he was waiting for a miracle – for a hand to come out of the clouds and take him down from the cross, and prove to the world, "I cannot watch my only begotten son being crucified. I sent him to save you, and you are misbehaving with my own son. Your behavior is unforgivable."

On the cross he shouted, looking at the sky when nothing was happening, "Father, have you forsaken me? Have you forgotten me?" Naturally, such a man cannot laugh. His life is going to be a life of continual frustrations. He expects too much.

Children can laugh because they don't expect anything. Because they don't expect anything, their eyes have a clarity to see things – and the world is full of so much absurdity, ridiculousness. There is so much slipping on banana peels that a child cannot avoid seeing it! It is our expectations which function like curtains on our eyes.

Because all the religions are against life, they cannot be for laughter. Laughter is an essential part of life and love. Religions are against life, against love, against laughter, against joy; they are against everything that can make life a tremendous experience of benediction and blessings.

Because of their antilife attitude, they have destroyed the whole of humanity. They have taken away all that is juicy in man; and their saints have become the examples for others to follow. Their saints are just dry bones: fasting, torturing themselves in many, many ways, finding new devices, new ways to torture their bodies. The more they have been torturing themselves, the higher they have risen in respectability. They have found a ladder, a way to become more and more respectable: just torture yourself, and people are going to worship you and remember you for centuries.

Self-torture is a psychological sickness. There is nothing to be worshipped in it; it is slow suicide. But we have supported this slow suicide for centuries because the idea has become fixed in our minds that the body and the soul are enemies. The more you torture the body, the more spiritual you are; the more you allow the body to have pleasure, enjoyment, love, laughter, the less spiritual you are. This dichotomy is the basic reason why laughter has disappeared from man.

He – did not love sufficiently: otherwise he would also have loved us, the laughers! But he hated and jeered at us, he promised us wailing and gnashing of teeth.

I have seen pictures of European churches in the Middle Ages. The preacher's function was to make people very much afraid of hellfire and the tortures that they would have to suffer there. Their descriptions were so vivid that many women used to faint in the churches. It was thought that the greatest preacher was the one who made the most people faint – that was a way to find out who was the greatest preacher.

The whole of religion is founded on a simple psychology: fear magnified in the name of hell, and greed magnified in the name of heaven. Those who are enjoying themselves on the earth are going to fall into hell. Naturally man becomes afraid – just for small pleasures, for only seventy years of life, he has to suffer in hell for eternity.

This was one of the reasons Bertrand Russell dropped out of Christianity and wrote a book, *Why I Am Not a Christian*. He said, "The first thing that made me decide was the absolutely unjustified idea that for my small sins I can be punished for eternity." He said, "If I count all the sins that I have committed according to the scriptures, and if I include the sins I have dreamt about – that I have not committed – the most strict judge cannot send me to jail for more than four and a half years. But for these small sins, I would not suffer for eternity. What kind of justice is this? There seems to be no relation between the crime and the punishment."

And then he started looking deeper into Christian theology. He was amazed to find so many things so absurd and ridiculous, that finally he decided that to remain a Christian is to show your cowardliness. He renounced Christianity and wrote the tremendously significant book, *Why I Am Not a Christian.*

Now it has been almost sixty or seventy years, and that book has not been replied to by any Christian theologian. In fact, there is no reply – how can you justify it? According to Christianity, man has only one life. If it was Hinduism, there may have been some justification – in millions of lives, so much sin can accumulate that perhaps one can visualize an eternal punishment. But for Christianity, or for Judaism, or for Mohammedanism, that idea is so ridiculous. And a man of the intelligence of Bertrand Russell... And the popes and the great Christian theologians all over the world have simply remained silent.

They have condemned Bertrand Russell, saying that he will go to hell. But that is not an argument. If there really is a hell and a heaven, hell will be a far healthier place than heaven because in heaven you will find all the dry bones, ugly creatures who have been called saints, torturing themselves. It is not a place worth visiting.

In hell you will find all the poets, all the painters, all the sculptors, all the mystics, all those people whose company is going to be a blessing. You will find Socrates there, and you will find Gautam Buddha there – Hindus have thrown him into hell because he did not believe in the Vedas, upon which the whole Hindu religion is based. You will find Mahavira because he did not believe in the Hindu caste system; he condemned it. You will find Bodhidharma, Chuang Tzu, Lao Tzu. You will find all the great people who have contributed to life – all the great scientists and artists who have made this earth a little more beautiful.

What have your saints contributed? They are the most futile people, the most unfertile. They have been just a burden, and they have been parasites; they have been sucking the blood of poor human beings. They were torturing themselves and teaching others to torture themselves; they were spreading psychological sickness.

If this earth looks so sick, if humanity looks so sad, the whole credit goes to your saints. In heaven you will meet all those ugly creatures, all those condemners who don't know how to love, who don't know how to laugh, who don't know how to sing, who don't know how to dance – who cannot allow humanity to have any pleasures, howsoever small. Pain seems to be spiritual, and pleasure seems to be materialistic.

Now modern psychiatry knows perfectly well that these saints were schizophrenic. They need not be worshipped. If you can find them somewhere, immediately take them to a psychiatric hospital – they need treatment. They are not healthy; their very existence is nauseous. But they have been the leaders of mankind, and they have made the whole of mankind feel a kind of nausea; they have created an atmosphere of nausea.

Does one then straightway have to curse where one does not love? That – seems to me bad taste. But that is what he did, this uncompromising man. He sprang from the mob.

And these saints were absolutely uncompromising. They were not even ready to listen. They were afraid to listen because deep down they knew their own doubts about their lives, about their religion.

I cannot conceive that Jesus must not have, somewhere deep in his mind, a doubt: Is he really the only begotten son of God? It is impossible for me to conceive... In fact, the more he repeats it, the more it becomes certain that his repetition is nothing but repressing his doubt. If he does not repeat it, there is fear – his doubt may surface. It is not to convince you; basically it is to convince himself.

It is a vicious circle: people convince others in order to be convinced themselves. When Jesus sees that a few people are convinced that he is the only begotten son of God, then his own doubt is repressed more deeply. He is convinced by other people's conviction. And he has to continually repeat it because to allow any long interval is dangerous – in that interval the doubt can arise.

Even your so-called great believers in God have deep doubts about God. In fact, belief is needed only to repress doubt; there is no other function of belief. You don't believe in the sun – or do you? You never shout from rooftops, "I believe in the sun," or "I believe in roseflowers," or "I believe in the moon."

People will say, "Just get down and do some useful work. Why are you wasting your time? We also believe in the sun, we also believe in the roseflower, there is no problem. Nobody needs the conviction."

But Jesus says to his followers, "Shout from the rooftops that the prophet you have been waiting for has come. Convince people that

your master is the only begotten son of God, that he has brought
a direct message from God. Go to the far corners of the earth and
convince people." Only when there is doubt, suspicion, is their conviction needed, belief needed, faith needed. I am a faithless man
because whatever *is* needs no faith. Whatever *is* needs knowing,
not believing.

All believers are deceiving themselves. The atheist is better than
the believers, but not very much because his atheism is also a kind
of belief – a negative belief. He has not known that God does not
exist – just as the believers have not known that God exists. They
have chosen positive belief. Somebody has a negative mind, he has
chosen the negative belief. But nobody seems to see the simple fact
that a man who is honest cannot have any kind of belief.

If there is doubt it is healthy because that doubt will trigger in
you a pilgrimage of search. That doubt is a question, it is an inquiry.
It will take you to the truth. And the moment you know, the question
of belief does not arise. You simply know it. But the so-called saints,
theologians, priests have been very uncompromising. Their uncompromising attitude has gone to the very logical extreme – they don't
even want to listen to anything that goes against their beliefs.

There are scriptures in Jainism and in Hinduism saying the same
kind of thing. One wonders, "What kind of religious people were
these?" In Jainism there are scriptures telling the Jainas: "Even if
you find a mad elephant chasing you, and death is certain, even
if you can save your life by entering a Hindu temple which is
just nearby, it is better to die, better to be killed by the mad elephant, than to take shelter in a Hindu temple." Such an uncompromising attitude!

The same is repeated in Hindu scriptures. Exactly the same,
word for word: "It is better to die, to be killed by the mad elephant,
but don't enter a Jaina temple to save your life."

What kind of religious people are these? What kind of religious
scriptures are these? What harm can the Jaina temple do to the
Hindu? Or what harm can the Hindu temple do to the Jaina?
The harm is that you might hear something that goes against your
faith that can disturb your belief. It is better to die, but not to be disturbed in your faith. And to me, a faith that can be disturbed is not
of any worth. Every faith will be disturbed unless it is your own
knowing – but then it cannot be called "faith."

...this uncompromising man. He sprang from the mob. The mob lives at the lowest level of intelligence.

Just the other day I received an arrest warrant from Kanpur. Ten Christian associations have filed a lawsuit against me because I have said that there are pornographic statements in the Holy Bible.

Rather than looking in the Holy Bible – ten Christian associations together, that means all the Christians of Kanpur... I cannot believe that man has passed beyond his primitiveness; or is he still primitive? Those statements are not mine! There are five hundred pages of pornography in the Holy Bible. I don't have to argue in the court; I just have to read the Holy Bible.

If they had any sense they would have demanded that those five hundred pages from the Bible be removed. If any intelligence was there... But intelligence seems to be very rare. This is the mob – retarded, unintelligent.

Just a few days ago there was a statement of Zarathustra that, "At the great noontide, at the highest peak of evolution of man, when the superman arrives, almost like a god, he will be ashamed of his clothes; he will be ashamed of hiding things. He would like to be an open book." If you meet Zarathustra somewhere, just tell him, "Don't let your god come to Pune because the police commissioner of Pune will not allow your god to be ashamed of his clothes!"

These pygmies, with no intelligence at all, go on trying to dominate the whole of mankind. And it is not only the Holy Bible – there are Hindu scriptures full of pornography, and no Hindu will raise the question. Not only in the scriptures is there pornography, in the temples of Khajuraho, in the temples of Puri, in the temples of Konarak, you will see such pornographic sculpture that it is almost unbelievable. What kind of people, what kind of mind, how repressed? Whole temples, thousands of statues, so ugly – you may not have even dreamt of such pornography.

People are allowed to dream; at least there is still freedom of dreaming! Freedom of expression does not exist anywhere. But if you go to Khajuraho, or Puri or Konarak you cannot believe it. What kind of sick minds must have made these temple statues? All kinds of group sex, all kinds of orgies are sculpted. It must have taken hundreds of years to make those temples. But nobody objects. And if you object, you are hurting somebody's religious feeling – immediately an arrest warrant appears in the court.

If what I have said is wrong, those people could have issued a statement, or written articles in the magazines, or challenged me to a discussion, saying, "We don't find anything pornographic in the Bible." But rushing to the court simply shows weakness, simply shows they are taking support from the powers of the government.

Just the other day I was informed that there was another case... For thirty years I have been in so many cases. In not a single case have they been able to prove anything against me because whatever I have said was in their scriptures.

If they want to put a case against anybody, it should be against those scriptures, their publishers. Those scriptures should be burned.

In Simla the other day, the high court judge – he must be an intelligent man because he said to the person who was saying that the whole of Himachal Pradesh, all the Hindus living in that state, are feeling very hurt by my statements – the judge said, "I am also living in Himachal Pradesh, and I am also a Hindu, and I don't feel at all hurt by his statements. So don't talk about all the Hindus of Himachal Pradesh. You simply talk about you. You are not the representative of the whole state. I also live here, I am not hurt. And the book was published twenty years ago. Where have you been for twenty years?"

It has gone into many editions in almost all the languages of the world.

And the judge looked at the book. There was the seal of the public library of Simla, so he asked the man, "Are you a member of the public library of Simla?" And he replied, "No." Then the judge said, "Then how could you get this book? Have you stolen it? This is not your book." And the man was silent. He must have stolen that book!

Great Hindus, great religious people! And my whole book is concerned with how to transform sexual energy into spiritual energy. I don't think any religious person can be offended by it. He should be happy.

The judge asked him – because the man was continually saying, "Our religious feelings are hurt because this man is saying that through sex you can reach to *samadhi*." The judge asked, "Have you tried it? And if you have not tried it, on what grounds are you saying that this man is wrong? First try.

"What does it have to do with Hinduism? Whether you are Hindu or Christian or Mohammedan, sexual energy is sexual energy, it has nothing to do with any religion. And if somebody is saying that there is a way to transform it into spirituality, you should be happy about it, rather than being angry and asking that this man be immediately arrested."

But it is very difficult to find such an intelligent judge because those judges also come from the mob. And they also see that their judgment should not go against the crowd, it should not go against the political party in power.

And he himself did not love sufficiently: otherwise he would not have been so angry that he was not loved. Great love does not desire love – it desires more.

Great love does not desire love – there is no need. It is already great love. It desires something even more, even higher than love. And that's what prayer is, or meditation is.

Love is very close to meditation, but still, the other person is there, and there is a dependency on each other. Total freedom is not possible – conceivable, but not possible. Only in meditation, when you are alone and overflowing with love, is there freedom and tremendous love.

Great love does not desire love – it desires something more. It has known love, now it wants to transcend even love. It wants to go a step higher. And love is the last step. Beyond it begins the world of godliness.

Avoid all such uncompromising men! They are a poor, sick type, a mob type: they look upon this life with an ill will, they have an evil eye for this earth.
Avoid all such uncompromising men! They have heavy feet and sultry hearts – they do not know how to dance. How could the earth be light to such men!

The day man forgets to laugh, the day man forgets to be playful, the day man forgets to dance, he is no longer man; he has fallen into a sub-human species. Playfulness makes him light. Love makes him light. Laughter gives him wings. Dancing with joy, he can touch the farthest stars, he can know the very secrets of life.

This laugher's crown, this rose-wreath crown: I myself have set this

crown on my head, I myself have canonized my laughter. I have
found no other strong enough for it today.

All the mystics have felt themselves very alone – their height
makes them very alone. The mob lives in the dark caves down in
the valley. They never come out of their caves.

Zarathustra the dancer, Zarathustra the light, who beckons with
his wings, ready for flight, beckoning to all birds, prepared and
ready, blissfully light-hearted:
Zarathustra the prophet, Zarathustra the laughing prophet, no
impatient nor uncompromising man, one who loves jumping and
escapades; I myself have set this crown on my head!...
You higher men, the worst about you is: none of you has learned to
dance as a man ought to dance – to dance beyond yourselves!
What does it matter that you are failures!

It is better to be a failure in a great thing than to be victorious in
a small thing – at least you tried! Even the failure in transcending
yourself is a great victory. The very effort, the very longing, brings a
transformation to you.

   ...*dance beyond yourselves!* That is the essential teaching of
Zarathustra. He declares himself as the laughing prophet.

How much is still possible! So learn to laugh beyond yourselves! Lift
up your hearts, you fine dancers, high! higher! and do not forget to
laugh well!
This laughter's crown, this rose-wreath crown: to you, my brothers,
do I throw this crown! I have canonized laughter; you Higher Men,
learn – to laugh!
"This is my morning, my day begins: rise up now, rise up, great
noontide!"
Thus spake Zarathustra and left his cave, glowing and strong, like a
morning sun emerging from behind dark mountains.

about osho

Osho's unique contribution to the understanding of who we are defies categorization. Mystic and scientist, a rebellious spirit whose sole interest is to alert humanity to the urgent need to discover a new way of living. To continue as before is to invite threats to our very survival on this unique and beautiful planet.

His essential point is that only by changing ourselves, one individual at a time, can the outcome of all our "selves" – our societies, our cultures, our beliefs, our world – also change. The doorway to that change is meditation.

Osho the scientist has experimented and scrutinized all the approaches of the past and examined their effects on the modern human being and responded to their shortcomings by creating a new starting point for the hyperactive 21st Century mind: OSHO Active Meditations.

Once the agitation of a modern lifetime has started to settle, "activity" can melt into "passivity," a key starting point of real meditation. To support this next step, Osho has transformed the ancient "art of listening" into a subtle contemporary methodology: the OSHO Talks. Here words become music, the listener discovers who is listening, and the awareness moves from what is being heard to the individual doing the listening. Magically, as silence arises, what needs to be heard is understood directly, free from the distraction of a mind that can only interrupt and interfere with this delicate process.

These thousands of talks cover everything from the individual quest for meaning to the most urgent social and political issues facing society today. Osho's books are not written but are transcribed from audio and video recordings of these extemporaneous talks to international audiences. As he puts it, "So remember: whatever I am saying is not just for you...I am talking also for the future generations."

Osho has been described by *The Sunday Times* in London as one of the "1000 Makers of the 20th Century" and by American author Tom Robbins as "the most dangerous man since Jesus Christ." *Sunday Mid-Day* (India) has selected Osho as one of ten people – along with Gandhi, Nehru and Buddha – who have changed the destiny of India.

About his own work Osho has said that he is helping to create the conditions for the birth of a new kind of human being. He often characterizes this new human being as "Zorba the Buddha" – capable both of enjoying the earthy pleasures of a Zorba the Greek and the silent serenity of a Gautama the Buddha.

Running like a thread through all aspects of Osho's talks and meditations is a vision that encompasses both the timeless wisdom of all ages past and the highest potential of today's (and tomorrow's) science and technology.

Osho is known for his revolutionary contribution to the science of inner transformation, with an approach to meditation that acknowledges the accelerated pace of contemporary life. His unique OSHO Active Meditations™ are designed to first release the accumulated stresses of body and mind, so that it is then easier to take an experience of stillness and thought-free relaxation into daily life.

Two autobiographical works by the author are available:
Autobiography of a Spiritually Incorrect Mystic,
St Martins Press, New York (book and eBook)
Glimpses of a Golden Childhood,
OSHO Media International, Pune, India

OSHO international meditation resort

Each year the Meditation Resort welcomes thousands of people from more than 100 countries. The unique campus provides an opportunity for a direct personal experience of a new way of living – with more awareness, relaxation, celebration and creativity. A great variety of around-the-clock and around-the-year program options are available. Doing nothing and just relaxing is one of them!

All of the programs are based on Osho's vision of "Zorba the Buddha" – a qualitatively new kind of human being who is able *both* to participate creatively in everyday life *and* to relax into silence and meditation.

Location
Located 100 miles southeast of Mumbai in the thriving modern city of Pune, India, the OSHO International Meditation Resort is a holiday destination with a difference. The Meditation Resort is spread over 28 acres of spectacular gardens in a beautiful tree-lined residential area.

OSHO Meditations
A full daily schedule of meditations for every type of person includes both traditional and revolutionary methods, and particularly the OSHO Active Meditations™. The daily meditation program takes place in what must be the world's largest meditation hall, the OSHO Auditorium.

OSHO Multiversity
Individual sessions, courses and workshops cover everything from creative arts to holistic health, personal transformation, relationship and life transition, transforming meditation into a lifestyle for life and work, esoteric sciences, and the "Zen" approach to sports and recreation. The secret of the OSHO Multiversity's success lies in the

fact that all its programs are combined with meditation, supporting the understanding that as human beings we are far more than the sum of our parts.

OSHO Basho Spa

The luxurious Basho Spa provides for leisurely open-air swimming surrounded by trees and tropical green. The uniquely styled, spacious Jacuzzi, the saunas, gym, tennis courts...all these are enhanced by their stunningly beautiful setting.

Cuisine

A variety of different eating areas serve delicious Western, Asian and Indian vegetarian food – most of it organically grown especially for the Meditation Resort. Breads and cakes are baked in the resort's own bakery.

Night life

There are many evening events to choose from – dancing being at the top of the list! Other activities include full-moon meditations beneath the stars, variety shows, music performances and meditations for daily life.

Facilities

You can buy all of your basic necessities and toiletries in the Galleria. The Multimedia Gallery sells a large range of OSHO media products. There is also a bank, a travel agency and a Cyber Café on-campus. For those who enjoy shopping, Pune provides all the options, ranging from traditional and ethnic Indian products to all of the global brand-name stores.

Accommodation

You can choose to stay in the elegant rooms of the OSHO Guesthouse, or for longer stays on campus you can select one of the OSHO Living-In programs. Additionally there is a plentiful variety of nearby hotels and serviced apartments.

www.osho.com/meditationresort
www.osho.com/guesthouse
www.osho.com/livingin

more books and eBooks by OSHO media international

The God Conspiracy:
The Path from Superstition to Super Consciousness

Discover the Buddha: 53 Meditations to Meet the Buddha Within
Gold Nuggets: Messages from Existence

OSHO Classics
The Book of Wisdom: The Heart of Tibetan Buddhism.
The Mustard Seed: The Revolutionary Teachings of Jesus
Ancient Music in the Pines: In Zen, Mind Suddenly Stops
The Empty Boat: Encounters with Nothingness
A Bird on the Wing: Zen Anecdotes for Everyday Life
The Path of Yoga: Discovering the Essence and Origin of Yoga
And the Flowers Showered: The Freudian Couch and Zen
Nirvana: The Last Nightmare: Learning to Trust in Life
The Goose Is Out: Zen in Action
Absolute Tao: Subtle Is the Way to Love, Happiness and Truth

The Tantra Experience: Evolution through Love
Tantric Transformation: When Love Meets Meditation

Pillars of Consciousness (illustrated)
BUDDHA: His Life and Teachings and Impact on Humanity
ZEN: Its History and Teachings and Impact on Humanity
TANTRA: The Way of Acceptance
TAO: The State and the Art

Authentic Living

Danger: Truth at Work: The Courage to Accept the Unknowable
The Magic of Self-Respect: Awakening to Your Own Awareness
Born With a Question Mark in Your Heart

OSHO eBooks and "OSHO-Singles"

Emotions: Freedom from Anger, Jealousy and Fear
Meditation: The First and Last Freedom
What Is Meditation?
The Book of Secrets: 112 Meditations to Discover the Mystery Within

20 Difficult Things to Accomplish in This World
Compassion, Love and Sex
Hypnosis in the Service of Meditation
Why Is Communication So Difficult, Particularly between Lovers?
Bringing Up Children
Why Should I Grieve Now?: facing a loss and letting it go
Love and Hate: just two sides of the same coin

Next Time You Feel Angry...
Next Time You Feel Lonely...
Next Time You Feel Suicidal...

OSHO Media BLOG
http://oshomedia.blog.osho.com

for more information

www. **OSHO** .com

a comprehensive multi-language website including a magazine, OSHO Books, OSHO Talks in audio and video formats, the OSHO Library text archive in English and Hindi and extensive information about OSHO Meditations. You will also find the program schedule of the OSHO Multiversity and information about the OSHO International Meditation Resort.

http://OSHO.com/AllAboutOSHO
http://OSHO.com/Resort
http://OSHO.com/Shop
http://www.youtube.com/OSHO
http://www.Twitter.com/OSHO
http://www.facebook.com/pages/OSHO.International

To contact OSHO International Foundation:
www.osho.com/oshointernational,
oshointernational@oshointernational.com